EXPLORING AND CELEBRATING THE EARLY CHILDHOOD PRACTITIONER

This exciting new book celebrates, interrogates and re-imagines the complex and demanding role of the Early Childhood Practitioner. Exploring the many different facets of the Early Childhood Practitioner's (ECP) role, it challenges normative constructions of practitioners and how they have been shaped by assumptions of history, culture and policy.

Drawing on a range of theoretical presumptions and debates, the chapters champion the multidimensional power and potentiality of the ECP, arguing for greater respect and recognition for a role that supports and enables at a crucial time in a child's life. With opportunities for reflection, key topics include:

- The specialist pedagogical expertise of the ECP
- The key role that ECPs play in the child's holistic wellbeing
- The ECP as diplomat across many professional contexts, effectively communicating with families and professionals
- The creative ECP, pushing traditional, normative boundaries of practice
- The ECP as so much more than they are customarily perceived as being.

This latest addition to the TACTYC series will be valuable reading for Early Years students – particularly on Masters level courses – as well as those working and researching in the Early Years sector.

Dr Carla Solvason is Senior Lecturer in the Department for Children and Families at the University of Worcester. She has a keen interest in ethical practice and respectful and sensitive approaches to research, areas in which she has published and presented widely.

Dr Rebecca Webb is Senior Lecturer in Early Years and Primary Education and a member of the Centre for Innovation and Research in Childhood and Youth, at the University of Sussex. Her research interests focus on pedagogies and practices of 'not knowing' and 'uncertainty'.

Research informed professional development for the early years
TACTYC (Association for Professional Development in Early Years)

The books in this series each focus on a different aspect of research in early childhood which has direct implications for practice and policy. They consider the main research findings which should influence practitioner thinking and reflection and help them to question their own practice alongside activities to deepen knowledge and extend understanding of the issues. Readers will benefit from clear analysis, critique and interpretation of the key factors surrounding the research as well as exemplifications and case studies to illustrate the research-practice or research-policy links. Supporting the development of critical reflection and up to date knowledge, the books will be a core resource for all those educating and training early years practitioners.

Exploring the Contexts for Early Learning
Challenging the school readiness agenda
Rory McDowall Clark

Building Knowledge in Early Childhood Education
Young Children are Researchers
Jane Murray

Early Childhood Education and Care for Sustainability
International Perspectives
Valerie Huggins and David Evans

Places for Two-Year-Olds in the Early Years
Supporting Learning and Development
Jan Georgeson and Verity Campbell-Barr

Racialisation in Early Years Education
Black Children's Stories from the Classroom
Gina Houston

Children's Empowerment in Play
Participation, Voice and Ownership
Natalie Canning

Exploring and Celebrating the Early Childhood Practitioner
An Interrogation of Pedagogy, Professionalism and Practice
Edited by Carla Solvason and Rebecca Webb

EXPLORING AND CELEBRATING THE EARLY CHILDHOOD PRACTITIONER

An Interrogation of Pedagogy, Professionalism and Practice

Edited by *Carla Solvason and Rebecca Webb*

LONDON AND NEW YORK

Cover image: © Getty Images

First edition published 2023
by Routledge
4 Park Square, Milton Park, Abingdon, Oxon, OX14 4RN

and by Routledge
605 Third Avenue, New York, NY 10158

Routledge is an imprint of the Taylor & Francis Group, an informa business

© 2023 selection and editorial matter, Carla Solvason and Rebecca Webb; individual chapters, the contributors

The right of Carla Solvason and Rebecca Webb to be identified as the authors of the editorial material, and of the authors for their individual chapters, has been asserted in accordance with sections 77 and 78 of the Copyright, Designs and Patents Act 1988.

All rights reserved. No part of this book may be reprinted or reproduced or utilised in any form or by any electronic, mechanical, or other means, now known or hereafter invented, including photocopying and recording, or in any information storage or retrieval system, without permission in writing from the publishers.

Trademark notice: Product or corporate names may be trademarks or registered trademarks, and are used only for identification and explanation without intent to infringe.

British Library Cataloguing-in-Publication Data
A catalogue record for this book is available from the British Library

Library of Congress Cataloging-in-Publication Data
Names: Solvason, Carla, editor. | Webb, Rebecca, 1963- editor.
Title: Exploring and celebrating the early childhood practitioner : an interrogation of pedagogy, professionalism and practice / edited by Carla Solvason & Rebecca Webb.
Description: Abingdon, Oxon ; New York, NY : Routledge, 2023. | Series: TACTYC | Includes bibliographical references and index.
Identifiers: LCCN 2022021627 (print) | LCCN 2022021628 (ebook) | ISBN 9781032072746 (paperback) | ISBN 9781032071992 (hardback) | ISBN 9781003206262 (ebook)
Subjects: LCSH: Early childhood teachers. | Early childhood education.
Classification: LCC LB1775.6 .E867 2023 (print) | LCC LB1775.6 (ebook) | DDC 372.21--dc23/eng/20220706
LC record available at https://lccn.loc.gov/2022021627
LC ebook record available at https://lccn.loc.gov/2022021628

ISBN: 978-1-032-07199-2 (hbk)
ISBN: 978-1-032-07274-6 (pbk)
ISBN: 978-1-003-20626-2 (ebk)

DOI: 10.4324/9781003206262

Typeset in Bembo
by SPi Technologies India Pvt Ltd (Straive)

CONTENTS

   Introduction   1
   Rebecca Webb and Carla Solvason

1 The emergence of the early childhood practitioner   5
   Rory McDowall Clark

2 Holding and keeping the child safe   18
   Rosie Walker

3 Developing parent partnerships   28
   Carla Solvason

4 Appreciating and practising empathy   41
   Angela Hodgkins

5 Valuing children with special educational needs and disability   53
   Samantha Sutton-Tsang

6 Re-imagining early childhood pedagogy   63
   Johanna Cliffe

7 Nurturing nature with(in) children (or 'George killed the worm')   73
   Kathleen Bailey

vi Contents

8 Embracing creativity in the early years   87
Jacqueline Young

9 Championing a *not knowing* pedagogy and practice   98
Rebecca Webb and Kathy Foster

10 Reconceptualising quality interactions   111
Hayley Preston-Smith

11 Recognising and surviving poverty within early childhood practice   123
Sandra Lyndon

Conclusion   136
Carla Solvason and Rebecca Webb

Index   *139*

INTRODUCTION

Rebecca Webb and Carla Solvason

A wide range of factors have cohered in many 'advanced' twenty-first century societies to assume that young children will spend at least some, or even most, of their waking hours before they begin an extended period of statutory schooling in some type of Early Childhood Education and Care (ECEC) provision. This is certainly the situation in England (UK) which provides the context for this edited collection, *Exploring and Celebrating the Early Years Practitioner*. Indeed, in England, there is currently a profusion of different types of ECEC provision. This broadly falls under either 'the maintained nursery sector', whereby a Local Authority has control and jurisdiction over the type and quality of provision or the 'non-maintained nursery sector' made up of a wide range of private and voluntary providers. All types of provision are regulated by the government and overseen by the Office for Standards in Education, Children's Services and Skills (OFSTED). Similarly, over the past decade, there has been a proliferation in the range of job titles and roles on offer for those employed within the ECEC sector whose remit it is to practise both care and education for the benefit and thriving of the young children in their charge.

The origins of this book are found in TACTYC-funded research about the current role and status of Maintained Nursery Schools in England that was carried out by the editors (see Solvason, Webb and Sutton-Tsang, 2020). A significant finding from the research came through the accounts of those working in the sector, concerning the demanding role of the Early Childhood Practitioner (ECP). The data presented them as hard working, flexible, talented, and passionately committed to the inclusive welfare and learning of all young children. The book is, therefore, a celebration of the breadth, range and complexity of the practices of the ECP subject. However, it is also a critique of ways in which the discourse of the ECP is all too often presented and read (particularly in some policy texts and regulation of the sector) through only a technicist lens, which can be overly prescriptive and reductive, and which fails to recognise a range of ECP subjectivities and the varied qualities that these bring to the role.

In response to so many of her recommendations for the sector being rejected, Nutbrown (2013, p. 8) constructs the ECP as historically and persistently seen as 'less than', when, in actuality and in the contributions to this edited volume, we see that EC practitioners are so much *more than*. We frame the paradoxical and juxtapositonal subjectivity of the ECP as both someone who 'merely' looks after and cares for children and someone who is required to have a multiplicity of capabilities, knowledges and embodiments to practice, within pedagogic and sociocultural milieux that advance *every* child's education despite the stifling landscape of 'school readiness' (McDowall Clark, 2017). In this way we point to a historical and cultural context for the ECP that accounts for stubbornly persevering ideas of them as simultaneously 'less than' and 'more than', depending upon the politically charged context within which they are referenced.

This book challenges normative constructions of the ECP and invites readers to question assumptions about the essentialising of roles, status and language. By doing this we aim to champion the multidimensional power and potentiality of the ECP, to demand greater respect and recognition for this talented practitioner who supports and enables at a time in a child's life that is recognised as crucial for their longer-term success and thriving in school and society. The book also valorises the idea of 'practice'. This is about discursively situating, describing and valuing the subjectivity of the ECP as the one who practises, and signifying the practice of educational research that underpins many of the chapters. We, therefore, construct 'practice' expansively, acknowledging the important attention given to consideration of this term by Biesta and Aldridge (2021). In so doing, we read practice as the serious business of habitual day-to-day ways of knowing, doing and being that warrant scrutiny and explanation. We recognise it as much more than just 'routine', in ways that are complex, situational, nuanced and can extend into the relational, the embodied and the material of the field of ECEC. This does not mean dismissing or not taking seriously the important location of the ECP within a discourse of professionalism (see Chapter 1). Rather it works to relocate professionalism and professionalisation within a mapping of practice in ways that are attuned to inclusivity and equity, paying especial attention to the different subjectivities of ECPs themselves.

The structure of the book

This edited collection draws upon a range of theoretical presumptions and debates to present knowledge of, and construct arguments concerning, a variety of aspects of the practice of the ECP. They each engage with a range of different ways of viewing the ECEC world. Some chapters are more discursive and abstract, whilst others rely strongly on recent empirical practice or practitioner data. Each helps us to know and understand the ECP a little more clearly.

Chapter 1, *The Emergence of the Early Childhood Practitioner*, by Rory McDowall Clark, charts historical shifts in the positioning of ECEC in England, locating these within gendered sociocultural assumptions of the ECP that have remained persistent through time, despite more recent attempts to 'professionalise' the workforce.

Chapter 2, *Holding and Keeping the Child Safe*, by Rosie Walker, explores the range and breadth of holistic skills and competencies of the ECP that enables value-driven, safeguarding practices to be fostered for the benefit and thriving of each child.

Chapter 3, *Developing Parent Partnerships*, by Carla Solvason, celebrates the expertise of the ECP in developing genuine, respectful relationship with parents that takes them seriously as experienced and knowledgeable partners in making decisions about the needs of the child.

Chapter 4, *Appreciating and Practising Empathy*, by Angela Hodgkins, interrogates literature and research findings, to champion the importance of empathy within EC practice. It recognises the emotional labour required of the ECP to provide an empathetic and attuned ECEC environment for the child and advocates for emotional support for practitioners, themselves, to enable them to sustain this.

Chapter 5, *Valuing Children with Special Educational Needs and Disability*, by Samantha Sutton-Tsang, considers the unique qualities of the ECP within the arena of Special Educational Needs and Disabilities (SEND), to acquire and hone expertise in supporting the extensively varied needs of individual children.

Chapter 6, *Re-imagining Early Childhood Pedagogy*, by Johanna Cliffe, traverses ECEC literatures that play with the metaphorical language of rhizomes and nomads, drawn from original work by Deleuze and Guattari (1987), enabling the (re)positioning of the ECP as complex, multifaceted and knowledgeable.

Chapter 7, *Nurturing Nature with(in) Children (or George killed the worm')*, by Kathleen Bailey explores ways that children and ECPs might engage with nature as part of everyday practice within and beyond institutional settings. Capturing a 'species-justice' story that explores children's notions of nature as part of everyday lived experiences, it demonstrates how the skill, knowledge and practice of the ECP is a key dynamic of 'intra-acting' ECEC processes and pedagogies.

Chapter 8, *Embracing Creativity in the Early Years*, by Jacqueline Young, charts successive ECEC initiatives over time in England that have recognised the importance of creativity. It draws on small-scale data to explore how some ECPs make sense of creativity and their own developing skills as creative pedagogues.

Chapter 9, *Championing a Not-Knowing Pedagogy and Practice*, by Rebecca Webb and Kathy Foster, uses a case study of one ECEC setting to explore ideas of transformational '*not knowing*' practice and pedagogy, to consider what ECPs believe this approach renders possible.

Chapter 10, *Reconceptualising Quality Interactions with Young Children*, by Hayley Preston-Smith, examines the notion of quality interactions, long championed within ECEC as a central expectation of the ECP. Re-examining her own data from a small-scale project, the author challenges essentialised views outlined in policy and framework documentation, in order to contest normative ideas of the ECP, demonstrating ways in which they can be 'so much more than'.

Chapter 11, *Recognising and Surviving Poverty within Early Childhood Practice*, by Sandra Lyndon, explores the context of poverty in the UK and how, despite early millennial aspirations to eradicate child poverty within a generation, the numbers of those living in poverty in 2022 are higher than ever. The notion of the 'poverty paradox' is explored, whereby ECPs work in an ECEC sector which is barely sustainable, as part of a low-wage workforce, and yet are assumed to be the solution to the alleviation of child poverty.

Finally, in the Conclusion, we reflect upon the complex and multifaceted figure of the ECP that the preceding chapters have presented for us and consider why this talented professional continues to receive so little recognition within the sociocultural context of England.

In various ways, each chapter aims to better 'know' or 'name' the ECP. In so doing, each celebrates, challenges, or re-imagines a taken-for-granted idea of the EYP, within the contemporary English ECEC context, drawing on different conceptual and substantive material taken from academic scholarship, practice experience and empirical research. Written by those who are, or have been, both researchers and practitioners, the chapters offer opportunities for reflection, reflexivity and critique so that the reader might recognise, or re-imagine and 'expand', the possibilities for the subjectivity of ECP. To this end, each chapter ends with a 'Reflection' section that presents the reader with opportunities to relate what they have read to their own context, in order to take seriously the interconnectedness of conceptual and the practical research with practice.

References

Biesta, G. & Aldridge, D. (2021). Special Section: Close to Practice Research, *British Educational Research Journal*, Vol. XLVII, No. 6. Wiley.

Deleuze, G., and Guattari, F. (1987, reprinted 2013). A thousand plateaus. London: Bloomsbury.

McDowall Clark, R. (2017). *Exploring the contexts for early learning: challenging the school readiness agenda*. Abingdon: Routledge.

Nutbrown, C. (2013). Shaking the foundations of quality? Why 'childcare' policy must not lead to poor-quality early education and care. Retrieved from: http://www.crec.co.uk/docs/Shaking_the_foundations_of_quality.pdf.

Solvason, C., Webb, R., and Sutton-Tsang, S. (2020). Evidencing the Effects of Maintained Nursery Schools' Roles in Early Years Sector Improvements. Available at https://tactyc.org.uk/research/

1
THE EMERGENCE OF THE EARLY CHILDHOOD PRACTITIONER

Rory McDowall Clark

Introduction

Many issues troubling Early Childhood Education and Care (ECEC) within advanced economies can be traced to fundamental ambivalence about the purpose of early childhood provision: whether part of the education system, preparing children for school, serving a social purpose, supporting struggling families, a service for working parents or part of the economic infrastructure. All these aspects are apparent in public discourse and although presented as a service for children, in reality, ECEC serves wider political agendas (McDowall Clark 2020). Such competing and contradictory priorities have implications for how the role of the Early Childhood Practitioner (ECP) is conceived. This chapter explores 'professionalism' within ECEC discourse; a particularly complex notion because of the fragmented, multifaceted nature of the field.

Within official policy, ECEC is envisaged not only as a foundation for educational success - increasingly significant in competitive, global economies (Biesta 2013) - but also as a means of encouraging parents into employment, thus reducing state spending on benefits and welfare (McDowall Clark 2020). This dual purpose fuels a growing focus on early childhood as politicians of all persuasions recognise ECEC as an investment. However, it is difficult, if not impossible, to reconcile both policy goals and reluctance to accept the costs of a wholly publicly funded service, which has led successive governments to promote growth in the private sector, shifting the cost of expanding provision away from the state. Greater attention has been offset by increased levels of scrutiny and accountability for outcomes measured against a legislated curriculum. Practitioners often struggle to align official assumptions and outcome measures with what they know of how young children thrive and may find pressure to conform to expectations at odds with their professional values. This chapter discusses emerging recognition of the need for well-qualified, knowledgeable ECPs, explores what professionalism means in this context and examines tensions and contradictions that arise within discourses of 'professionalisation'.

What makes a profession 'professional'?

> I tell people I'm an early years professional and they don't know what it is.
> *(Deputy Manager, cited in Murray 2009)*

Most people associate 'professions' with lawyers, doctors and similar occupations that carry social status and respect; few think in terms of EC practitioners who are likely to encounter misunderstanding of their position and responsibilities. The general perception of a professional is someone skilled and proficient, with expert knowledge and a formal qualification; yet the experience of the Deputy Manager above suggests that some professions are somehow more professional than others. This graduate, with a first degree in psychology and officially conferred professional status, explained:

> So I say I work in a nursery, but people look down on that, especially school-teachers, whose attitude is that you're somehow 'lower' than them.

The experience of this ECP highlights two important aspects of a profession: that it is recognised by others and that it carries some measure of public esteem. These facets of professionalism are interconnected but arise from different sources. The first, widespread acknowledgement is dependent on officially recognised status, whereas public esteem for an occupational group is shaped, through time, by discourse and social values.

Working with young children encompasses countless roles, job titles and working environments which makes establishing what constitutes professionalism in the field especially complex. In addition, a proliferation of pathways and qualifications has led to a pervasive terminology of professionalism, whilst leaving the question of what it means in early years contexts unresolved (Urban and Dalli 2008). Another issue that exacerbates the devaluing of ECPs compared to, for instance, school teachers, is a persistent conceptual divide between care and education, grounded in the historical roots of different kinds of provision. Although officially eliminated in the Childcare Act (DfES 2006), this notional split lingers, reflected in confusing government terminology where 'early learning' and 'childcare' are used interchangeably (Archer 2016).

The term *Early Childhood Education and Care* (ECEC) is intended to acknowledge that with young children 'care' is necessarily educational, and 'education' must be caring if it is to be effective. Nonetheless the (false) perception that caring is a lesser activity than educating, a 'natural' disposition rather than requiring skilled expertise, can undermine claims to professionalism in public consciousness. Indeed,

Lloyd and Hallett (2010) propose that efforts towards professionalisation might have strengthened rather than resolved the historical and philosophical divide between care and education. The legacy of care discourses further disadvantages certain sectors of the workforce; for instance, it suggests a lower status for those who merely 'care' for babies and toddlers (McDowall Clark and Baylis 2012). Childminders, too, have difficulty in being perceived as professionals; despite qualifications; many are frustrated at being considered 'babysitters' and inferior to nurseries (Social Mobility Commission 2020).

A major stumbling block to professional recognition is the strongly gendered (feminised) nature of the workforce. Women fought for many years to gain entry to such professions as medicine and law but looking after children has always been viewed as 'women's work' and, as such, lacked respect and recognition. Today it is still seen as particularly suitable for girls due to their supposed 'natural' and 'innate' attributes; Colley (2006) asserts this is especially true for working class girls who compensate for limited educational options by utilising their 'emotional labour'. This perspective of the workforce recasts skill and proficiency as 'motherly instinct', innate to women, and thus quite the reverse of professionalism. The discourse of maternalism is deep-rooted and Ailwood (2008) traces historical links between women's labour and ECEC to the influence of Froebel. Froebel's insistence that play is crucial to children's learning has influenced practice across the world; sadly his belief that a 'lovely, womanly disposition' (Froebel, cited in Ailwood 2008) is essential for a kindergarten teacher has proved equally enduring.

Strongly connected to the gendered image of ECP as mother-substitute is the affective dimension of the work the emotional commitment to young children that is an indispensable component of forming effective relationships. Moyles (2001) contends that this paradox of passion' shapes views of early years practice as a 'low-level operation in which children receive care but which negates or rejects education' (2001, p. 82). This dichotomy between care and education, already noted, creates persistent tension between rationality and emotionality (Skattebol et al. 2016) and, as these attributes are already highly gendered, with men traditionally viewed as 'rational' in opposition to women's 'emotional' nature, work that entails emotional connection can seem less than professional. Such associations are contested by Taggart (2011) who argues that the 'moral seriousness' of work with young children should be seen as 'a central plank of professionalism' (2011, p. 85).

Such socially mediated ideas have led Urban and Dalli (2008, p. 132, emphasis in the original) to describe EC professionalism as 'a *discourse* as much as a *phenomenon*: something that is constantly under reconstruction'. Certainly, the social power of hegemonic, or normalising, discourses is reflected in the low percentage of men working in early years. Osgood (2010) suggests that the 'hyper-feminine' appearance of ECEC may explain why it is viewed as lacking in professionalism and stresses the importance of maintaining female affective values against the threat of increasing technocratic practice. 'Affective values' are not the sole preserve of women however, and I argue elsewhere that it is time to move beyond gendered debates in discussing professionalism (McDowall Clark and Murray 2012). Attributing characteristics such as emotional warmth and 'ethic of care' (Gilligan 1989) to a predominately female workforce risks confusing cause and effect and of misconstruing ECEC values as gendered ones. In practice male ECPs express similar attitudes to their work as do their female colleagues, as the male practitioner below exemplifies:

> You need to have an emotional drive, you can't work with little ones and be a robot – you must have emotion and attachment ... it's the passion of practitioners that will drive professionalism forward...
> ('Daniel', interviewed in McDowall Clark and Murray 2012, p. 65)

Locating emotional commitment to children in women's 'nature', rather than integral to the moral purpose of the role, devalues the professionalism of the sector; it also marginalises caring men. It is not helpful to think in terms of male (rational) and female (emotional) qualities because to fully tune into children is to combine both of these domains, as Moyles (2001, p. 90) affirms, 'for practice to reach professional status both head and heart have to meet at the interface of reflection'.

Professionalism is, therefore, part of how one acts on a daily basis, but traditionally a range of features has been understood to distinguish a profession from a job or occupation. Amongst these are aspects of training; specialised knowledge and skills; ethical practice and autonomy (McDowall Clark and Baylis 2010). Specialised training, knowledge and skills, in particular, distinguish ECPs from stereotypes of well-meaning girls who are 'good with children', and this is where the emphasis has lain in measures to professionalise ECEC and raise the status of working with under-5s.

The difference that qualified practitioners make

An official inquiry into early years provision thirty years ago identified the connection between quality and well-qualified staff. ('Quality', being a culturally derived and value-laden term, is difficult to determine; it is examined in Chapter 11, so I shall not debate it here.) The subsequent Rumbold Report (DES 1990) called for a national framework to integrate different strands of provision, identifying the need for well-qualified graduate staff to implement this. Subsequently, the Start Right Report (Ball 1994, p. 72) argued strongly for 'well trained staff of the highest quality' to 'bring the UK into line with normal practice in most other countries'. The report stressed that 'the double competence required of early years teachers – *especially* the mastery of an applicable theory of learning development – makes just as intense a professional demand on students as does the mastery of disciplines required of all teachers' (p. 79, original emphasis). A rapid growth in early childhood degrees followed these reports.

Evidence of the *lasting* benefits of well-qualified staff initially appeared in the *Effective Provision of Pre-school Education (EPPE)* project (Sylva et al. 2004), a longitudinal study of 3000 children. EPPE research indicated that educators with specialised training and higher education qualifications are more likely to respond effectively to children, elicit their ideas, provide stimulating interactions and engage in the 'sustained shared thinking' that supports cognitive development (Siraj-Blatchford et al. 2002). What is more, it proposed that the benefits of high-quality ECEC continue as children grow older, resulting in improved educational attainment throughout secondary school (Sylva et al. 2014). This enormously influential research impacted on many subsequent policy initiatives.

EPPE findings were corroborated by the *Millennium Cohort Study* (Mathers et al. 2007), which confirmed that quality is significantly enhanced in maintained settings and those with a qualified teacher; and that conversely, a high proportion of unqualified staff has negative effects on quality. Further evaluation of specialised graduate professionals reached similar conclusions, indicating that 'the qualification level of the whole staff team was significantly related to quality' (Mathers et al. 2011, p. 2). Both reports, written in response to government initiatives to professionalise ECEC, focused on the Private, Voluntary and Independent (PVI) sector, where qualifications are more variable and the proportion of graduate staff is lower than in maintained settings. A range of research suggests that the presence of graduates is especially significant for disadvantaged children (Sylva et al. 2014; Hillman and Williams 2015; Bonetti and Blanden 2020), and children's outcomes, measured by Key Stage 1 and 2 tests (age 7 and 11), reinforce EPPE's claims that benefit continues through to later schooling (Bonetti and Blanden 2020).

Although Bonetti and Blanden (2020, p. 14) remark that the mechanisms by which qualifications impact quality and outcomes are still not fully explained, it is likely that the boost to children's development provided by graduate ECPs can be explained by their deeper knowledge and understanding of appropriate pedagogies (Siraj-Blatchford et al. 2002). Young children require opportunities for meaningful and active engagement with adults who can support them to become confident, autonomous learners. A high level of expertise is necessary to identify and build on children's interests, to assess and monitor linguistic, cognitive and socio-emotional development and to provide relevant, experiential opportunities.

Mounting evidence thus supports investment in high-quality early years services staffed by well-qualified ECPs. Even policy makers with no interest in pedagogy or provision may be swayed by the potential economic benefits. Heckman (2006) maintains that investment in ECEC is the most cost-effective strategy for economic growth, benefitting society as a whole. He argues that not only does ECEC stimulate children's desire and ability to learn, so raising school achievement, but that it also reduces the need for costly interventions later. Recognition that well-qualified practitioners are central to achieving a number of government goals has been a key driver in moves to professionalise the sector, although the underpinning neoliberal perspective, whereby young children are viewed as 'human capital' to be prepared for a future labour market, is problematic (McDowall Clark 2017).

The evolution of professionalism within ECEC

In 1997 'New Labour' came to office with an ambitious programme for early years provision, including a National Childcare Strategy; establishment of the Sure Start initiative and publication of *Curriculum Guidance for the Foundation Stage* (QCA 2000) and *Birth to Three Matters* (Sure Start 2002), both later subsumed into the *Early Years Foundation Stage (EYFS)*. Deliberate attempts were made to integrate early years education and welfare traditions, tackling the split between education and care. In particular, 'joined-up' working across all agencies concerned with children and families, as advocated in the landmark green paper *Every Child Matters*, was made statutory in the Childcare Act (DfES 2006). All these substantially raised the profile of ECEC making the need for skilled and knowledgeable practitioners imperative and led to an upsurge in pathways to gain or upgrade qualifications. In an attempt to clarify the variety of working roles and qualifications, in 2005 the Children's Workforce Development Council was set up and two years later introduced a formal process by which graduates working with young children could gain 'professional' recognition. This new position, named Early Years Professional Status (EYPS), though not the same as Qualified Teacher Status (QTS) was promoted on a par with it. The government promised an Early Years Professional (EYP) in every registered setting by 2015 with two in the most disadvantaged areas, which would see 'transformation from largely unqualified to graduate level leadership in less than 10 years – a process that has taken other professions more than 50 years to achieve' (Hevey 2010, p. 161).

This reform agenda was broadly welcomed by experienced practitioners for its formal recognition of their work in leading practice across the EYFS (Hadfield et al. 2012). By June 2012 there were 9365 EYPs (Nutbrown 2012) whose pedagogical leadership and modelling of exemplary practice would ensure high quality, graduate-led provision. Nonetheless there were underlying concerns from the beginning and, despite EYPs reporting it had improved their sense of professional status; 91% felt 'people outside the early years sector did not understand it' (Hadfield et al. 2012, p. 6). The title for this pedagogue role was confusing for many, including parents and carers, and use of the word *professional* for select practitioners risked 'othering' those less qualified or non-accredited (Fenech and Sumsion 2007). As accredited status rather than a qualification, lack of recognition for EYPS was exacerbated by it being confined to the PVI sector in order to address persistently lower qualification levels in those settings, as this hindered a cohesive approach across different provision types. By far the greatest difficulty however was the marked disparity in pay and working conditions between EYPS and QTS; many warned that beyond putting money into training, thought must be paid to sustainability, or else 'the role of early years professional could just wither and die' (Murray 2009).

In an independent review of qualifications, Nutbrown (2012) recognised EYPs' dissatisfaction that promised parity with qualified teachers had failed to materialise. As well as calling for a robust Level 3 qualification as the minimum for staff to count in ratios, the *Nutbrown Review* recommended a specialist Early Years teaching qualification focusing firmly on pedagogy. Such a qualification would cover birth to seven years, ensuring continuity from the Foundation Stage through to Key Stage 1. Very few of the report's recommendations were adopted, in particular the call for specialised Early Years QTS; instead the government introduced Early Years Teachers (EYT), claiming it would 'give one title of "teacher" across the early years and schools sectors which will increase status and public recognition' (DfE 2013, p. 43). This response, largely perceived as simply 'changing the label on the tin' (Nutbrown 2013), was met with widespread frustration.

By this time there had been a change of government and official response to the Nutbrown Review, ironically named *More Great Childcare* (MGC), was in keeping with a different political ideology and greater emphasis on free market principles and cost-cutting. Wild et al. (2015) compared Nutbrown's stress on developing children's independent, enquiring minds with MGC's view of qualified staff as a means of enabling settings to offer a greater number of places and focus on preparation for school. Teachers' Standards (Early Years) replaced the EYPS and although the government's *Early Workforce Strategy* (DfE 2017) held out the possibility that EYTs and those with EYPS might be able to lead nursery and reception classes in maintained schools, the promised consultation was dropped. Nutbrown's (2013) fear that one form of inequality would be replaced by another has been realised.

Bringing EYT standards into line with other Teaching Standards resulted in narrowing their focus compared to the more holistic requirements of EYPS. Most importantly the standards completely disregard the crucial role of play in young children's learning and development; instead, the expectation that EYTs engage with curricula and teaching at Key Stages 1 and 2 suggests the value of their role is in how it supports later schooling. Such standards inevitably shape learning opportunities offered to young children as well as teacher training itself (McDowall Clark 2017), for instance, official insistence on systemic synthetic phonics affects how literacy is conceived. Redrafting professional standards has also done nothing to address disparity in working conditions and pay scales and Traunter (2019) questions whether in reality EYTS serves to professionalise or de-professionalise the workforce. When entry requirements and expectations are the same as for qualified teachers, yet there is so much discrepancy in the rewards, there is little incentive to enter the ECEC workforce, and the number of people enrolling in Early Years Initial Teacher Training (EYITT) has plummeted. It seems that:

> Far from ameliorating societal challenges and structural disadvantages within the sector, it now appears that government policies have had the effect of further destabilising recruitment, suggesting that lack of parity of professionalism, pay, progression and status can actively suppress policy aspirations.
> *(Kay et al. 2021, p. 191)*

Introduction of a *National Professional Qualifications Framework for Early Years Leadership* is unlikely to address these issues. The NPQEYL is aimed at 'leaders qualified to at least Level 3' (DfE 2021, p. 7), unlike previous initiatives that focused on graduates, and despite a promise that it would focus on "'early years pedagogy and practice' (Oxtoby 2021) the main thrust of expectations within this framework is managerial and organisational. Mention of 'marketing strategies' and 'income generation activities to maximise funding streams' (DfE 2021, p. 25) signals a neoliberal, marketised view of professionalism where 'quality' is measured by outcomes and value for money.

The NPQEYL framework exemplifies underlying contradictions in official moves to professionalise ECEC. Moss (2009) points out that market principles are not easily applied to ECEC; the connection between quality and higher staff qualifications makes it hard to envisage how a childcare market can drive up quality at the same time as driving down costs. Despite affirmative gestures towards professional recognition over the past two decades, there remains a 'lack of correspondence between the early years sector and government' (Education Policy Institute, EPI 2017). The EPI goes on to warn that the crisis in recruitment and high dropout rate is symptomatic of a much larger problem that requires a shift in outlook and treatment.

So where to next? Meeting the professional challenge

Despite two decades of initiatives to raise the profile of ECPs, considerable challenges regarding their status operate at both macro- and micro-level. At macro-level a manifest issue is sustainability of the workforce in the light of habitual underfunding and failure to value the crucial role of skilled practitioners. Recent reports from the Social Mobility Commission (2020), the Sutton Trust (Archer and Merrick 2020; Pascal et al. 2020) and the Early Years Workforce Commission (2021) all recognise a recruitment and retention crisis and acknowledge the threats to quality posed by the current environment. Recommendations from these reports focus on improving both conditions and perceptions, and whilst the Social Mobility Commission recognises it 'will take a monumental effort to change the perception of an entire sector' (2020, p. 4), they stress the need to portray ECEC as a real professional choice rather than a 'fall-back option for low achievers' (ibid, p. 57). Revising Nutbrown's (2012) recommendation for an Early Years specialist QTS with conversion courses for existing EYP/EYT graduates, advocated by Archer and Merrick (2020) and Pascal et al. (2020), would support this prospect; and both reports call for a Leadership Quality Fund to support graduate recruitment. Increased levels of investment are clearly needed if the full potential of ECEC is to be realised, and the Early Years Workforce Commission (2021, p. 22) recommends coupling realistic pay with 'changing the narrative' to avoid the damaging discourse of childcare undermining professionalism. They suggest that financial and developmental incentives, combined with positioning the sector as a phase within the education journey rather than a means of enabling parents to work, could 'create a virtuous cycle' with potential to positively change public perception.

Equally frustrating for many working in ECEC is tension between top-down control and government directives and the autonomy necessary to exercise judgement and make independent decisions that is an integral factor of ECEC professionalism (McDowall Clark and Baylis 2010). It is ironic that as emphasis on higher qualifications for ECPs grew, so too did the constraints placed on their practice. This contradiction has been fuelled by official focus on ECEC as preparation for school, making practitioners accountable for tightly defined outcomes and leaving little room for professional expertise. Whilst the concept of 'readiness for school' is attractive to policy makers, too early a start to formal learning is misguided and counterproductive (McDowall Clark 2017) as exemplified by the educational success of those nations that introduce formal schooling much later. A conflict of values is apparent, one in which official policy is focused on the child as potential human capital, whereas for ECPs children's well-being as individuals *in the present* is central. Human capital discourse seeks to manage performance in order to ensure the 'best possible input/output equation' (Lyotard 1984, p. 63), thus curbing professional autonomy and self-regulation. The result, Lyotard argues, is 'performativity' whereby professionals 'perform' professionalism to meet expectations of external observers. ECPs' practice is increasingly constrained by performativity, as the need to provide satisfactory data subverts child-centred pedagogical values (Roberts-Holmes 2015). Alongside attacks on pedagogy, the early years curriculum has also become instrumentalised with the notion of curriculum as something to be 'delivered', constructing ECPs as technicians whose task is to transfer knowledge into the heads of passive children. Such perspectives 'offer a diminished view of professionalism, and one that compromises high-quality ECEC' (Fenech et al. 2010, p. 89).

Yet if, as Urban and Dalli (2008) propose, professionalism is constantly under reconstruction, then it is at the micro-level of enacting pedagogy and curriculum that professionalism may best be actualised. ECEC professionalism must exist beyond mechanical calculation of inputs and outputs in pursuit of predetermined outcomes. Working with young children is complex and unpredictable, so ECPs need to exercise professional judgement that is contingent and relational rather than a means to an end. Means are not neutral so the nature of this judgement is moral; therefore, it follows that education must be recognised as a moral rather than a technical practice (Biesta 2007). ECEC is underpinned by values that combine moral purpose and an ethic of care, requiring reflective integrity and relational interdependence (McDowall Clark and Murray 2012). These values can enable ECPs to reclaim 'professionalism', grapple with contradictory discourses and to resist data-driven pedagogy (Roberts-Holmes 2015).

There are implications here for early childhood teacher education because official expectations of ECEC permeate professional standards and teacher training requirements. It is vital that ECPs have opportunities to articulate and conceptualise their pedagogy, to develop a culture of critical enquiry and a sense of agency, so as to equip them with self-belief and confidence to advocate for young children; without this, ECEC courses are simply a channel for centrally determined practices (McDowall Clark 2017). Warning against a loose application of the term professional, whereby a good professional is reduced to one who meets regulatory standards, Fenech et al. (2010) call for professionalism to be re-imagined and practised from the ground-up rather than top-down. They advocate 'resistance-based professionalism as a useful strategy by which early childhood teachers can design and produce alternative knowledges about quality' (ibid. p. 91).

Summary and conclusion

Over recent decades young children have become a key focus for policy, but valuing ECEC as a commodity rather than for its benefit to children themselves has hindered recognition of practitioners' professionalism. Difficulty lies in lack of consensus regarding the purpose of provision; not only are official expectations at odds with those of practitioners in the field, but government priorities are themselves contradictory, and this has repercussions for official perception of ECPs. After some years of progress, the current situation has become critical and the impact of neoliberal political ideology is apparent in the government's backtracking from previous commitments, failure to properly invest in the sector and their over-reliance on market forces. Thus, policy aspirations continue to be inhibited by material circumstances, such as lack of parity in staff pay and conditions, putting sustainability at risk.

It is not only material inequality that impedes perceptions of ECPs; denigration of what was customarily viewed as unskilled work, drawing on 'natural' female disposition, also contributes. Acknowledging this emotional slant, Moyles (2001) terms practitioners' characteristic passion and commitment the 'paradox' of professionalism, asserting the need to harness this force for critical reflection that can challenge political prescription. Indeed, 'passionate care for furthering the well-being of children is an ethically active, professional orientation, not a domestic concept of care' (McDowall Clark and Murray 2012, p. 31) as Angela Hodgkins further discusses in Chapter 4. This value base provides guidance for practice, empowering a professional voice and enabling the articulation of 'alternative knowledges' (Fenech et al. 2010, p. 91). Such initiative is crucial as, first in schools and now within ECEC, increasing regulation holds settings accountable in order to achieve policy goals, inducing the 'terror of performativity' (Ball 2003) and undermining professional autonomy. Biesta (2007, p. 19) argues that externally imposed views of 'effective' practice that disregard moral questions and restrain practitioners' professional judgement leave a 'democratic deficit'. He urges us to keep in mind that the relationship between policy and practice requires deliberation and challenge. Since ECEC is such a contested area, it will continue to be subject to political change; so, whilst remuneration and status are significant considerations, it is through their ability to speak up for pivotal values and to advocate for young children that ECPs earn their entitlement to be deemed 'professional'. ECEC is steeped in contradictions and competing agendas; professionalism lies in the capacity to navigate these tensions.

> **REFLECTIVE POINTS**
>
> - To what extent would you consider professionalism as a process, – i.e. something you enact; or an achievement, – i.e. something you earn and possess? Where does a sense of professionalism derive from and why is it important for ECEC practitioners?
> - What is your view of 'resistant professionalism' (Fenech et al. 2010)? Consider the supports and constraints that affect how you respond to formal expectations and interpret official policy in working with children and families.

References

Ailwood, J. (2008) Mothers, teachers, maternalism and early childhood education and care: some historical connections, *Contemporary Issues in Early Childhood*, Vol 8(2): 157–165.

Archer, N. (2016) *Entitlement or commodity? Tensions between universalism and marketisation in English early childhood education*. Available at www.tactyc.org.uk/reflections

Archer, N. and Merrick, B. (2020) Getting the Balance Right. Report for the Sutton Trust. Available at: https://www.suttontrust.com/our-research/getting-the-balance-right/

Ball, C. (1994) *Start right: the importance of early learning*, London: Royal Society of Arts.

Ball, S. (2003) The teacher's soul and the terrors of performativity, *Journal of Education Policy*, Vol 18(2): 215–228.

Biesta, G. (2007) Why "what works" won't work: evidence-based practice and the democratic deficit in educational research, *Educational Theory*, Vol 57(1): 1–22.

Biesta, G. (2013) Interrupting the politics of learning, *Power and Education*, Vol 5(1): 4–15.

Bonetti, S. and Blanden, J. (2020) *Early Years workforce qualifications and children's outcomes*, London: Educational Policy Institute.

Colley, H. (2006) Learning to labour with feeling: class, gender and emotion in childcare education and training, *Contemporary Issues in Early Childhood*, Vol 7(1): 15–29.

Department of Education and Science (DES) (1990) *Starting with quality: report of the committee of enquiry into the quality of educational experience offered to three and four year olds* (Rumbold Report). London: DES/HMSO.

Department of Education and Skills (DfES) (2006) *The childcare act 2006*, London: HMSO.

Department for Education (DfE) (2013) *More great childcare*, London: DfE.

Department for Education (DfE) (2017) *Early years workforce strategy*. Available at: https://www.gov.uk/government/publications/early-years-workforce-strategy

Department for Education (DfE) (2021) *National Professional Qualifications Framework for Early Years Leadership*. Available at: https://assets.publishing.service.gov.uk/government/uploads/system/uploads/attachment_data/file/1057342/National_Professional_Qualification_for_Early_Years_Leadership.pdf

Education Policy Institute (EPI) (2017) *Analysis – developing the early years workforce: what does the evidence tell us?* Available at: https://epi.org.uk/publications-and-research/analysis-developing-early-years-workforce-evidence-tell-us/

Early Years Workforce Commission (2021) *A workforce in crisis: saving our early years*. Available at: https://www.pacey.org.uk/Pacey/media/Website-files/Non-PACEY%20documents%20(PDFs)/a-workforce-in-crisis-saving-our-early-years.pdf

Fenech, M., Sumsion, J. and Shepherd, H. (2010) Promoting early childhood teacher professionalism in the Australian context: the place of resistance, *Contemporary Issues in Early Childhood*, Vol 11(1): 89–105.

Fenech, M. and Sumsion, J. (2007) Early childhood teachers and regulation: complicating power relations using a Foucauldian lens, *Contemporary Issues in Early Childhood Education*, Vol 8(2): 109–122.

Gilligan, C. (1989) *Mapping the moral domain: a contribution of women's thinking to psychological theory of education*, Cambridge, MA: Harvard University Press.

Hadfield, M., Jopling, M., Needham, M., Waller, T., Coleyshaw, L., Emira, M. and Royle, K. (2012) *Longitudinal study of early years professional status: an exploration of progress, leadership and impact*. Available from: https://www.gov.uk/government/uploads/system/uploads/attachment_data/file/183418/DfE-RR239c_report.pdf

Hillman, J. and Williams, T. (2015) *Early years education and childcare: lessons from evidence and future priorities*. Available at: http://www.nuffieldfoundation.org/sites/default/files/files/Early_years_education_and_childcare_Nuffield_FINAL.pdf

Heckman, J. (2006) Skill formation and the economics of investing in disadvantaged children, *Science*, Vol 312(5782): 1900–1902.

Hevey, D. (2010) Developing a new profession: a case study, *Literacy Information and Computer Education Journal*, Vol 1(3): 159–167.

Kay, L., Wood, E., Nuttall, J. and Henderson, L. (2021) Problematising policies for workforce reform in early childhood education: a rhetorical analysis of England's early years teacher status, *Journal of Education Policy*, Vol 36(2): 179–195.

Lloyd, E. and Hallet, E. (2010) Professionalising the early childhood workforce in England: work in progress or missed opportunity? *Contemporary Issues in Early Childhood*, Vol 11(1): 75–86.

Lyotard, J-F (1984) *The post-modern condition: a report on knowledge*, Minneapolis: University of Minnesota Press.

Mathers, S., Sylva, K. and Joshi, H. (2007) *Quality of Childcare Settings in the Millennium Cohort Study*, Research Report SSU/2007/FR/025. Nottingham: DCSF Publications.

Mathers, S., Ranns, H., Karemaker, A.M., Moody, A., Sylva, K., Graham, J. and Siraj-Blatchford, I. (2011) *Evaluation of Graduate Leader Fund: Final report*, Department for Education.

McDowall Clark, R. (2017) *Exploring the contexts for early learning: challenging the school readiness agenda*, Abingdon: Routledge.

McDowall Clark, R. (2020) *Childhood in society for the early years* (4th ed.), London: Sage.

McDowall Clark, R. and Baylis, S. (2010) Early years professionals: leading for change, in *Reflective practice in the early years*, M. Reed and N. Canning (eds) London: Sage, pp. 156–171.

McDowall Clark, R. and Baylis, S. (2012) 'Wasted down there': policy and practice with the under-threes, *Early Years: An International Journal of Research and Development*, Vol 32(2): 229–242.

McDowall Clark, R. and Murray, J. (2012) *Reconceptualising leadership in the early years*, Maidenhead: Open University Press.

Moss, P. (2009) *There are alternatives! Markets and democratic experimentalism in early childhood education and care.* Working Paper No. 53. The Hague, Netherlands: Bernard van Leer Foundation and Bertelsmann Stiftung.

Moyles, J. (2001) Passion, paradox and professionalism in early years education, *Early Years*, Vol 21(2): 81–95.

Murray, Janet. (2009) The poor professionals, *The Guardian*, 28 April.

Nutbrown, C. (2012) *Foundations for quality: the independent review of early education and childcare qualifications.* Final Report. Available at: www.gov.uk/government/publications/nutbrown-review-foundations-for-quality

Nutbrown, C. (2013) *Shaking the foundations of quality? Why 'childcare' policy must not lead to poor-quality education and care.* Available at: http://www.shef.ac.uk/polopoly_fs/1.263201!/file/Shakingthefoundationsofquality.pdf

Osgood, J. (2010) Reconstructing professionalism in ECEC: the case for the 'critically reflective emotional professional', *Early Years*, Vol 30(2): 119–133.

Oxtoby, K. (2021) Department of Education launches new early years leadership qualification, *Early Years Educator*, 18 October.

Pascal, C., Bertram, T. and Cole-Albäck, A. (2020) *Revisiting the Nutbrown Review: policy and impact.* Available at: https://www.suttontrust.com/wpcontent/uploads/2020/08/Early_Years_Workforce_Review_pdf

Qualifications and Curriculum Authority (QCA) (2000) *Curriculum guidance for the foundation stage*, London: QCA and DfEE.

Roberts-Holmes, G. (2015) The 'datafication' of early years pedagogy: 'if the teaching is good, the data should be good and if there's bad teaching, there is bad data', *Journal of Education Policy*, Vol 30(3): 302–315.

Siraj-Blatchford, I., Sylva, K., Muttock, S., Gilden, R. and Bell, D. (2002) *Researching Effective Pedagogy in the Early Years (REPEY)*, DfES Research Report 356. London: DfES, HMSO.

Skattebol, J. Adamson, E. and Woodrow, C. (2016) Revisioning professionalism from the periphery, *Early Years Journal*, Vol 36(2): 116–131.

Social Mobility Commission (2020) *The stability of the early years workforce in England: an examination of the national, regional and organisational barriers.* Available at: www.gov.uk/government/publications/the-stability-of-the-early-years-workforce-in-england

Sure Start (2002) *Birth to three matters: a framework to support children in their earliest years*, London: Sure Start Unit.

Sylva, K., Melhuish, E.C., Sammons, P., Siraj-Blatchford I. and Taggart, B. (2004) *The effective provision of pre-school education (EPPE) project: final report*, London: DfES and Institute of Education, University of London.

Sylva, K., Melhuish, E., Sammons, P., Siraj, I. and Taggart, B. (2014) *Students' educational and developmental outcomes at age 16: effective pre-school, primary and secondary education* (EPPSE 3–16) project, DfE RR354, London: DfE.

Taggart, G. (2011) Don't we care? The ethics and emotional labour of early years professionalism, *Early Years*, Vol 31(1): 85–95.

Traunter, J. (2019) Reconceptualising early years teacher training: policy, professionalism and integrity, *Education 3-13*, Vol 47(7): 831–841.

Urban, M. and Dalli, C. (2008) Editorial, *European Early Childhood Research Journal*, Vol 16(2): 131–133.

Wild, M., Silberfeld, C. and Nightingale, B. (2015) More? Great? Childcare? A discourse analysis of two recent social policy documents relating to the care and education of young children in England, *International Journal of Early Years Education*, Vol 23(3): 230–244.

2
HOLDING AND KEEPING THE CHILD SAFE

Rosie Walker

Introduction

During recent years there has been extensive change within Early Childhood Education and Care (ECEC). This includes increasing global recognition as a key driver of social, educational, economic and civic success (Cheeseman, 2019; Pascal and Bertram, 2019) with attendant professionalisation of the workforce (Reed and Walker, 2017). The result has been a plethora of legislation and guidance relating to education (GOV.UK, 2017), and well-being of young children (DfE, 2020), including in relation to developing child agency (Bolin, 2019). Some key changes include those related to early intervention (House of Commons Library, 2019), integrated working (Nicholas, 2014), and the Early Years Foundation Stage (EYFS) curriculum (DfE, 2017) as well as a national statutory framework of inspection (Ofsted, 2021). Advances in the understanding of neuroscience has seen expansion of infant and toddler childcare provision that responds to concerns about the social and educational attainment gap for children experiencing poverty or other forms of disadvantage (Mathers et al., 2014). Cameron and Moss (2020) point towards endemic problems within childcare provision as it currently operates, arguing for the need for urgent transformation.

Safeguarding has had its share of change, as have measures taken to protect and promote the well-being of children. For this chapter, I use the *Working Together to Safeguard Children* (DfE, 2018, p. 7) definition of safeguarding, which stipulates:

- Protecting children from maltreatment;
- Preventing impairment of children's mental and physical health or development;
- Ensuring that children grow up in circumstances consistent with the provision of safe and effective care;
- Taking action to enable all children have the best outcomes.

DOI: 10.4324/9781003206262-3

Several high-profile Serious Case Reviews (the process used to examine failures in the UK child protection system) have led to a shift towards an 'explicitly child-centred' approach (Parton, 2011, p. 6) where the distinctive needs of the child are considered paramount, where particular attention is to be paid to the voice of the child and where advocacy work and ethical practices are built in to what happens. In addition, an emphasis on interventions whereby problems can be recognised and dealt with early on has been recommended. The idea of this is to prevent a crisis which may later require intensive and costly engagements and changes (Allen, 2011). Partnership working with parents and collaborative working within and between settings, ECPs and other professionals have also been flagged as 'best practices'. The COVID-19 pandemic and a cost of living crisis have provided new challenges for keeping children safe. This has been recognised in a recent report from the Children's Commissioner for England (2020), and it has highlighted existing inequalities children are facing and those with the poorest life chances who have borne the brunt of the impact from the pandemic. This leads to knock-on effects for ECEC provision and practice.

ECEC is enmeshed in the production of global data that measures quality driven by economic imperatives (Cheeseman, 2019). Hunkin (2019) explores the dilemmas of undervaluing and under-resourcing ECEC, whilst trying to meet the holistic and individual needs of children. Managing complex systems of accountability and budgets, whilst providing collaborative practice that ensures children, families and communities are prioritised, is difficult. However, this now needs to take place in the context of stringent statutory demands on the ECP in relation to child protection and safeguarding. ECPs must therefore embrace multifaceted and demanding agendas and be adaptable, amenable and alert to a political agendas and policy shifts.

The early years stage is paramount

New demands and complexity highlight the necessity for novel ways of thinking and working, particularly with regard to keeping and holding children safe. The 'early years' is a period of radical and phenomenal development (Mathers et al., 2014), which means that the role of the ECP is crucial for managing changes that might improve the life chances of vulnerable children. This means embracing a vision of the ECP as focused upon social justice, equal rights, and outcomes for young children based on participatory and inclusive practices, prioritised above and beyond other statutory demands and pressures. This way of thinking needs time and space to emerge, where ECPs are enabled to take a 'life course approach' (World Health Organisation, 2000, p. 4), considering possible future trajectories for children in their charge and planning for these. This transformational approach can sustain the ECP in their multifaceted role, paying attention to flux in a rapidly changing world (Walker, 2017). Transformational practitioners need to move forward in a future that requires critical thinking with mindfulness to achieve a sense of 'self-actualisation' (Walker, 2017). Such a way of thinking and being can sustain practitioners over the course of their careers and meet the requirements of the ever-growing complexity of the ECEC landscape, with children's needs placed at the forefront of thinking.

The diagram in Figure 2.1 demonstrates the components needed for a new way of conceptualising ECEC practice and of keeping children safe. It should be viewed as a kaleidoscope where the four quarters of the circle form a lens to focus on the boxes behind. Thus, life course, social justice, social pedagogy and critical thinking work together to form a framework of sustainable practice where children can realise their potential. This model can be used to frame thinking about future practice and ensure support networks whereby children are held safe.

Practitioner development encompasses the need for awareness of the context in which they work, including understanding systems of oppression and inequity, as well as taking a stance with social justice at its heart, recognition that social inequality is endemic in society and of the systems of power, oppression and privilege that keep this in play. ECPs have a distinct role in embedding principles of equality and equity through understanding the children with whom they work and promoting learning through first-hand pedagogical activities (Mistry and Soud, 2013). Children require a creative approach that will support them appropriately and keep them safe, not just within the early years but over their life course.

A life course approach to EC pedagogy (Hutchison, 2004; WHO, 2000) is designed to improve outcomes for children and young people, particularly as they make important transitions at sensitive times in their lives. It is based on understanding the many factors that affect development over the lifespan and effective responses shaped by interdependent relationships within the social and cultural context. As Shogren and Wittenburg (2020, p. 19) highlight, such an approach provides 'a lens through which to view the multiple services and support needs during

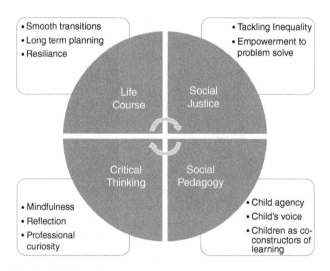

FIGURE 2.1 Professional practice.

the transition to adulthood' and allows a focus on longer-term goals for children. Planning early for transitions from one stage of a child's life to the next can enable potential issues to be identified and planned for in a proactive rather than a reactive manner. A life course approach enables cohesive, long-term strategies for transitions from early years to school, school to adult, bridging the present with the past and providing an aid in planning.

As part of the life course approach, practitioners take a holistic approach to meeting children's needs. ECPs are ideally placed to hold and keep the child safe due to their close working with children and their families, compared to other phases of education. Because of this they can identify when families might require support and intervention to avert a crisis. ECPs work in close parent partnership through the key worker system (Elfer et al., 2011), taking responsibility for a group of children and as the first point of contact for parents. Practitioners work closely with their families; so are able to identify developmental and learning needs that can alter children's life course trajectories. An example of this concerns a child so well known to the key worker that she could tell when he was struggling with home life as his voice would be raised several octaves when he came into nursery. The key worker was able to check when the mother came to collect the child if all was well at home and timely, appropriate support could be sought and put in place before a crisis emerged.

The life course approach advocates that children's voices be heard within systems which provide opportunities and constraints for them. The Rights of the Child Agenda (UNICEF, 1989) has influenced this approach and intensified global awareness of the rights of children to: resources to support a healthy life; protection from harm; and to participate and have a say in matters that affect them. The United Nations Rights of the Child highlighted some gaps in health and education outcomes which need initiatives for children to thrive worldwide. In relation to this, the life course approach recognises key times in a person's life when a difference can be made by healthy outcomes during the life span. For example, in early childhood a good diet, prompt healthcare and building resilience will have a beneficial effect throughout life. Recognising and acting on children's diverse experiences is essential for promoting positive life trajectories.

An effective way of working with the diversity of children's experience is a social pedagogy approach, which champions inclusive practice and uses education to enable problem-solving, self-awareness and self-actualisation. Social pedagogy emphasises relationships between children and practitioners and the importance of listening and communicating. This way of working requires a strong ECP identity. Hans Thiersch (cited in Schugurensky, 2014) argues that the role of the social pedagogue is to help people to analyse a situation, reflect collectively and critically on the social causes of individual problems and to find options for successful everyday life. Helping children to problem solve and research is an important way of building coping skills and confidence to speak out if they feel they are in way of harm.

The critical thinking social pedagogue

Social pedagogues are reflective practitioners, constantly examining their own practice to apply both theoretical knowledge and self-knowledge to the challenging demands that confront them. To explore this approach in more depth, I investigated whether ECPs still used the critical thinking they developed during Early Years degree courses in their practice, and whether this thinking had been enhanced, adapted or challenged as they progressed through their career (Walker, 2017). An interpretive, qualitative approach using a focus group was used to collect the views of six alumni who completed their degrees in 2014 and subsequently became leaders of practice. Respondents defined critical thinking as a personal and professional process that included learning how to think, work with others, effectively communicate and practice ethically. This was very much at the heart of their work. They identified these dispositions as essential to ensure that children are at the forefront of thinking and practice. Respondents felt that they had a strong impetus to sustain critical thinking because of their role in advocating for children. By this they meant being a voice for children, supporting decision-making and ensuring a child's rights were respected and their views heard. They explained:

> Critical thinking develops because you are putting the child at the heart of your practice, and this is the impetus for developing criticality.
>
> *(Anna)*
>
> We cannot lose sight of our remit or vocation that is about the child, and we have to have that understanding at the heart of all we do.
>
> *(Emily)*

Keeping a focus on the child encompasses challenging social injustice and driving change for children as young citizens (Boylan and Dalrymple, 2009). Keeping children safe, as defined earlier in the chapter, is a fundamental part of a practitioner's role; because of this they constantly examine their practice and apply theoretical knowledge, including self-knowledge, to the challenging demands that confront them. Rather than following predetermined procedures, irrespective of context or circumstance, they use theoretical, practical and self-knowledge to understand why something has happened and how best to respond. They take account of circumstances before forming a judgement or making a decision, aware that there are few universal answers: everything depends on the particular context.

Data suggested that this group of practitioners felt critical thinking is 'not enough' to ensure children are kept safe. To advocate successfully, practitioner and personal identities needed to accommodate mindfulness which participants defined as having belief in oneself and one's ability to take responsibility and assume control of events. Such a disposition emerges through confidence, trusting oneself and others and being able to work collaboratively. For example, this participant reflected on the demands that challenged mindfulness as an approach.

> You have to think on your feet and react on your feet very quickly every day – the amount of times we do that is quite scary to add up.
>
> *(Davina)*

The ability to not rush to making judgements, particularly in safeguarding situations, by stepping back to think out the appropriate actions within complex situations, is crucial. Practitioners can do this by being aware of their emotions and using these to formulate a response; this requires time and space. Alongside this, to be able to regulate and assimilate possible action alongside verbal and non-verbal cues from young children requires drawing upon practical and theoretical knowledge. They need to use all available knowledge to come to decisions This means processing information, reviewing alternatives and, importantly, understanding and managing their own viewpoints and emotions through self-regulation so that critical thinking emerges productively (Noone, Bunting and Hogan, 2016).

Jenny commented:

> Safeguarding is arguably one of the biggest requirements placed upon us as practitioners working with children and young people today, and we have a duty of care and a responsibility to keep the most vulnerable within our society safe. We have to quickly assimilate all the information to hand as well as make sure we are not putting our own bias onto a situation.

Anna added:

> Being an early years practitioner carries a lot of responsibility and I don't carry this lightly. We have to see ourselves as upskilling and enriching the system around the child. Asking the right questions and making your own decisions based on what you know and analysing and critiquing what you see and what you know and putting the two together.

The impact of outcomes must be considered in ensuring that the needs of children and families are met effectively. This requires developing a value-based ECP identity, empowered through a mindfulness approach founded upon being an advocate for children. The comments of research participants give a sense of practitioner and personal responsibility that transcends qualification, status and low financial reward. Rather, they highlight a sense of purpose, passion and validation, through personal connection and a sense of fulfilment. This sense of knowing oneself and one's contribution, and being able to articulate it, underpinned by evidenced-based knowledge and a set of beliefs and attitudes about childhood, affords self-actualisation for the ECP as a critical thinker. Taken together with a life course and social pedagogy approach as visualised in Figure 2.1, it provides a powerful way to hold and keep children safe.

How do practitioners make this model work?

Not only does mindfulness enable ECPs to have better understanding, but it also helps protect them from the demands and potentially high levels of stress of working within the children's sector, and a commitment to safeguarding young children beyond a technical response. Research amongst practitioners following a part-time degree programme whilst simultaneously employed investigated how they develop the complex mix of competencies, dispositions and skills inherent in their practice (Walker, Reed and Sutton-Tsang, 2017). Data suggests that practitioner identity is not static but develops over time as their confidence grows through understanding the evidence-base of practice and the theory behind it. It also appears to be shaped by meeting the complex challenges and regulatory requirements within the workplace: in other words, finding ways through the system and making it work for the benefit of children. ECPs felt they had gained the ability to critically evaluate practice, in particular, by appreciating the child's perspective and those of parents and colleagues. Phillips and Bond's (2004, p. 293) notion of developing an 'institutional culture of inquiry' with a safe space to explore issues and ask questions within settings is of key importance here. It extends not only to ECPs but to children as well, for example, 'Pedagogy in Participation' (Formosinho and Figueiredo, 2014 p. 397) where children co-construct their own learning and celebrate their successes. Such a culture encourages democracy, development of strong identities and humanity, opening doors to the power of knowledge, problem-solving and strength to speak up. These attributes of pedagogy of participation contribute to a social justice approach to keeping children safe.

Review and conclusion

This chapter has considered the complexity and diversity of the current landscape of practice in early years practice. The need for new ways of thinking which can accommodate the welter of demands placed on the ECP in holding and keeping children safe has been discussed. Being an advocate for children and families, speaking up on their behalf and encouraging their own sense of future success must be seen by ECPs as key to children's security. Being a competent and confident practitioner involves acquiring knowledge, gaining a voice, striving for ethical practice and developing a professional and personal identity within a vigilant community of practice. The research cited suggests that practice flourishes and should be celebrated within the context of ECPs embedded in the culture of their own settings, where they can care, be committed, and have clear values regarding ECEC. Many ECPs are already able to navigate the tricky waters of safeguarding but adopting a framework of life course, social justice and social pedagogy can give them a clearer vision of their own practice within a complex and fast-changing political context. Criticality, and mindfulness, provides ECPs with a sustainable, deeper layer of thinking, to achieve self-actualisation to meet the challenges of holding and protecting children.

> **REFLECTIVE POINTS**
>
> Consider your own experiences of holding and keeping children safe:
>
> 1. How has your thinking about your own safeguarding practice changed over time and why?
> 2. What are the most effective processes and practices you have experienced for holding children safe? What makes you say this?
> 3. Do you ever struggle to identify a course of action? How might Figure 2.1 support you and your colleagues to work out what you need to consider?

References

Allen, G. (2011). Early intervention: The next steps: An independent report to Her Majesty's Government. HM Government. https://assets.publishing.service.gov.uk/government/uploads/system/uploads/attachment_data/file/284086/early-intervention-next-steps2.pdf (Accessed 3 February 2021).

Bolin, A. (2019). Organizing for agency: Rethinking the conditions for children's participation in service provision. *International Journal of Qualitative Studies on Health and Well-Being, 13*(sup1), 1–10.

Boylan, J. and Dalrymple, J. (2009). *Understanding advocacy for children and young people.* Maidenhead, Berkshire: McGraw-Hill Education.

Cameron, C. and Moss, P. (2020). *Transforming early education in England.* London: UCL Press.

Cheeseman, S. (2019). 'Engaging with data to foster children's learning,' in Cheeseman, S., and Walker, R. (eds.) *Thinking about pedagogy in early education: Pedagogies for leading practice.* Oxford: Routledge, pp. 3–17.

Children's Commissioner. (2020). Childhood in the time of Covid. https://www.childrenscommissioner.gov.uk/wp-content/uploads/2020/09/cco-childhood-in-the-time-of-covid.pdf (Accessed 4 January 2021).

DfE. (2017). *Statutory framework for the early years Foundation Stage: Setting the standards for learning, development and care for children from birth to five.* https://assets.publishing.service.gov.uk/government/uploads/system/uploads/attachment_data/file/596629/EYFS_STATUTORY_FRAMEWORK_2017.pdf (Accessed 4 January 2021).

DfE. (2018). Working together to safeguard children. London: HMSO. https://assets.publishing.service.gov.uk/government/uploads/system/uploads/attachment_data/file/942454/Working_together_to_safeguard_children_inter_agency_guidance.pdf (Accessed 2 November 2020).

DfE. (2020). Keeping children safe in education. https://assets.publishing.service.gov.uk/government/uploads/system/uploads/attachment_data/file/954314/Keeping_children_safe_in_education_2020_-_Update_-_January_2021.pdf (Accessed 4 January 2021).

Dornan, P. and Woodhead, M. (2015). How inequalities develop through childhood: Life course evidence from the young lives cohort study. UNICEF. https://www.unicef-irc.org/publications/pdf/idp_2015_01(2).pdf (Accessed 4 January 2021).

Eichsteller, G. and Holthoff, S. (2011). 'Conceptual Foundations of Social Pedagogy: a Transnational perspective from Germany', in Cameron, C. and Moss, P. (eds.) (2017) *Social pedagogy and working with children and young people: Where care and education meet.* London: Jessica Kingsley Publishing, pp. 33–53.

Elfer, P., Goldschmied, E. and Selleck, D. (2011). *Key persons in the nursery: building relationships for quality provision*. London: Routledge.

Formosinho, J. and Figueiredo, I. (2014). Promoting equity in an early years context: the role of participatory educational teams. *European Early Childhood Education Research Journal*, 22(3): 397–411.

GOV.UK. (2017). Schools: statutory guidance. https://www.gov.uk/government/collections/statutory-guidance-schools (Accessed 4 January 2021).

House of Commons Library. (2019). Early intervention. https://researchbriefings.files.parliament.uk/documents/CBP-7647/CBP-7647.pdf (Accessed 4 January 2021).

Hunkin, E. (2019). *The quality agenda in early childhood education*. Palgrave: Macmillan.

Hutchison, E. (2004). *A life course perspective*. London: SAGE.

Mathers, S., Eisenstadt, N., Sylva, K., Soukakou, E. S. and Ereky-Stevens, K. (2014). Sound foundations. A review of the research evidence on quality early childhood education and care for children under three. http://www.rch.org.au/uploadedFiles/Main/Content/ccch/PCI_Report_Sound-Foundations.pdf (Accessed 14 December 2020).

Mistry, M. and Soud, K. (2013). Challenges of developing pedagogy through diversity and equity within the new Early Years Foundation (EYFS) curriculum. *Journal of Pedagogic Development*, 3(3): 42–47.

Nicholas, A. (2014). 'Integrated working in practice: Why don't practitioners talk to each other?' in Reed M. and Walker, R. (eds.) *A critical companion to early childhood*. London: SAGE, pp. 269–281.

Noone, C., Bunting, B. and Hogan, M.J. (2016). Does mindfulness enhance critical thinking? Evidence for the mediating effects of executive functioning in the relationship between mindfulness and critical thinking. In Frontiers in Psychology. 19. http://journal.frontiersin.org/article/10.3389/fpsyg.2015.02043/full (Accessed 10 January 2021).

Ofsted. (2021). Education inspection framework. https://www.gov.uk/government/publications/education-inspection-framework/education-inspection-framework (Accessed 4 January 2021).

Parton, N. (2011). Child protection and safeguarding in England: changing and competing conceptions of risk and their implications for social work. *British Journal of Social Work*, 41(5): 854–875. http://eprints.hud.ac.uk/11817/1/PartonChild.pdf (Accessed 16 February 2021).

Pascal, C. and Bertram, T. (2019). 'Pedagogic System Leadership within complex and changing ECEC Systems', in Cheeseman, S. and Walker, R. (eds.) *Thinking about pedagogy in early education: Pedagogies for leading practice*. Oxford: Routledge, pp. 182–204.

Phillips, V. and Bond, C. (2004). Undergraduates' experiences of critical thinking. *Higher Education Research & Development* 23(3): 277–294.

Reed, M. and Walker, R. (2017). Reflections on professionalism: Driving forces that refine and shape +professional practice. *JECER*, 6 (2): 177–187.

Shogren, K. and Wittenburg, D. (2020). Improving outcomes of transition-age youth with disabilities: A life course perspective. *Career Development and Transition for Exceptional Individuals*, 43(1): 18–28.

Schugurensky, D. (2014). Social pedagogy and critical theory: A conversation with Hans Thiersch. *International Journal of Social Pedagogy*, 3 (1): 4–14.

UNICEF. (1989). Convention on the rights of the child. https://www.unicef.org/child-rights-convention (Accessed 4 January 2021).

Walker, R. (2017). Learning is like a lava lamp: The student journey to critical thinking. *Research in Post-Compulsory Education*, 22 (4): 495–512. doi:10.1080/13596748.2017.1381293

Walker, R. Reed, M. and Sutton-Tsang, S. (2017). Effect on students from attending a university degree programme run in partnership with further and higher education institutions. *Journal of Further and Higher Education*. ISSN 0309-877X Online: 1469-9486.

World Health Organisation. (2000) The implications for training embracing a life course approach. https://www.who.int/ageing/publications/lifecourse/alc_lifecourse_training_en.pdf (Accessed 10 November 2020).

3
DEVELOPING PARENT PARTNERSHIPS

Carla Solvason

Introduction

This chapter explores the occasionally thorny area of parent partnership in education. Current emphasis on parent partnership, particularly within the early years, is by no means a recent phenomenon. The value of educationalists working with parents was highlighted in 1967, in the Plowden Report (CACE, 1967), although those old enough to have experienced the ensuing years in school may be aware that parents were not exactly welcomed with open arms. My mother has spoken many times of being 'shouted at' by the head teacher for being in the wrong place at the wrong time in my own primary school (during the 70s). Working with parents during their child's early education, based upon concepts of the parent as the child's first (Vygotsky, 1978) and most enduring educator, is now a universally respected conceptual framing; but how settings interpret their role in this can be challenging and result in vastly different behaviours.

Across all four nations of the United Kingdom, Early Childhood Education and Care (ECEC) curricula specify the importance of parent partnership: from an expectation to *engage* with parents in England (DfE, 2017); to developing a *positive partnership* with parents in Wales (Welsh Government, 2015); establishing *strong, sensitive relationships* in Scotland (The Scottish Government, 2009, p. 4) and *effective partnerships between parents and practitioners* in Ireland (National Council for Curriculum and Assessment, 2009) the general aim remains the same. But, what is also constant across these policy directives is lack of detail advising practitioners *how* these relationships can, or should, be developed effectively, making this a challenging requirement for some EC settings and practitioners.

In this chapter I share examples of expertise in evolving parent partnerships that have emerged from research with a range of settings, celebrating this as yet another complex skill of talented ECPs. I discuss why and how ECPs, particularly those

DOI: 10.4324/9781003206262-4

working in situations of adversity, build trusting relationships with parents of the children in their care, despite multiple challenges of disadvantage, including (but not limited to) poverty, domestic abuse, mental health, addiction, and special educational needs and disability (SEND). The data demonstrate how the ECPs interviewed were able to create trusting, mutually supportive relationships with parents and families, built upon authentic ideas of care.

Please note that although the term 'parent' is used throughout, this term is not limited to biological parents, and does not by any means reflect assumptions of a 'nuclear family'. The term is used to include anyone, from grandparents to foster parents or even siblings, who takes on a care role for the wellbeing of the child.

The development of concepts of parent partnership

The UK idea of parent partnership became firmly embedded within education during the New Labour period of government, at the turn of the twenty-first century. During this time ECEC was recognised as an effective means of breaking the poverty cycle in poorer families (Solvason, Webb and Sutton-Tsang, 2020a). Also during this period, the education system was framed by a marketization agenda, with accountability and performance indices becoming increasingly significant. Ball astutely predicted this shift in our education system in 1990:

> Schools are to become businesses, run and managed like businesses with a primary focus on the profit and loss account. The parents are now the customer, the pupils in effect the product. Those schools which produce shoddy goods, it is believed, will lose custom. And it would appear that in the government's view shoddy goods mean 'poor' results in national tests.
> *(Ball, 1990, p. 11)*

During New Labour's time in power, government funded research, such as that of Siraj-Blatchford et al. (2002), made bold statements claiming that 'settings that encouraged continuity of learning at home had better cognitive outcomes' (p. 99) and that 'it is the involvement in learning activities at home that is more closely associated with better cognitive attainment in the early years' (p. 101). With this, the onus of responsibility for children's educational success shifted. First, from the state and local authority-led education system towards the individual school as an independent business; and then from schools to parents. After all, as Siraj-Blatchford et al.'s (2002) research asserted, parents were pivotal to the success of both the child and the wider school.

In this way the role of parent changed from *supporting* educators, by simple actions, such as: ensuring punctuality; providing correct resources; encouraging discipline and providing the occasional note in reading records, to them becoming key players in their child's educational development. Henricson (2003, p. 2) recognised the 'deep-seated implications' that parents' involvement in their child's education had on society's perception of parenting and viewed this as just one of many steps that New Labour took in its 'rapid escalation in the range and scale of parenting interventions' (ibid., p. 3). The concept of distributed responsibility was further perpetuated through policy developments such as *Every Child Matters* (DfE, 2004), which spearheaded the idea that responsibility for the child's wellbeing was shared by the family and a wider team of professionals, including the ECP.

Since the early 2000s, the perceived benefits of home-school relationships for pupils, teachers and parents have been widely researched and published (for example: Callanan et al., 2017; Desforges and Abouchaar, 2003; Early Education, 2015;; Reynolds et al., 2015; Sylva et al., 2004). It is worth noting that despite extensive research evidence making clear links between early education and longer-term benefits for children (particularly those in poverty), as Rory has discussed in the opening chapter, the emergence of increased, suitable (and affordable) ECEC in the UK during this period did not reflect this. EC provision remains fragmentary, complex to navigate and unevenly distributed across the UK. Lewis and West (2013) suggest that this reluctance to establish consistent, universal ECEC is due to government ministers' fondness for the antiquated dogma that the mother's rightful place is raising children in the family home.

In 2009, Siraj-Batchford et al. made clear that children's outcomes are improved when there is 'strong parental involvement, especially in terms of shared education aims' (p. 26). The 2017 version of the Statutory Framework for the *Early Years Foundation Stage* (EYFS) (DfE) clearly stipulates that practitioners are to work in 'partnership' with parents. This point is repeated no less than thirty-three times, but we remain at a stage where, although parent partnership is considered central to decision making about the child, 'the mechanisms that support or hinder such involvement are not clearly delineated' (Hartas, 2008, p. 140). Yet regardless of how unclear guidance may be, the responsibility for making this relationship successful is still felt by practitioners, many of whom receive little or no training in the socio-emotional skills required for this complex task, especially in the case of parents of children with SEND (Broomhead, 2013, p. 174). With the limited experience of many practitioners, and the normative demands of the UK educational systems putting pressure to 'succeed' on both parents and ECPs, the potential for this relationship to encounter difficulties, and the temptation to locate blame in the actions of the other, is considerable.

Haines Lyon (2018) discusses how a 'good' parent behaves in very specific ways to support their child's education. Equally, Ramaekers and Suissa's (2011) work argues that a narrow view of parenting commodifies parents, removing their agency as human beings. The picture of parental involvement that we most often see in the UK is that of docile acquiescence with those requirements placed upon them by the schooling system (Solvason, Cliffe and Bailey, 2019). Responsibilities still include providing costumes and updating reading records, but they also increasingly entail fulfilling complex homework tasks and learning activities at home. Despite the 'parents as partners' rhetoric, those who do not passively comply, and instead, bring their own, perhaps contradictory ideas to the equation, are frequently viewed as ill-informed and a 'problem' (Baquedano-López et al., 2013). This was clearly demonstrated during the COVID-19 pandemic when parents who prioritised their children's emotional health over academic development were blamed for failing to adequately educate their children and for *allowing them* to fall behind on their expected indicators of achievement (Sellgren, 2020). Alexander (2009) reasons that this enduring, deficit view of parents serves to drive a wedge between home and school, rather than bringing parents and practitioners together into a fruitful partnership.

Literature suggests that the relationship between parents of children with SEND and practitioners has potential to be even more fraught. The language used is often negative and even combative when exploring communication between parents and teachers in this context. For example, in Hess, Molina and Kozleski's (2006) research, the terms: conflict, frustration, unhappiness, struggles, dissatisfaction and resistance are used to describe the parent–practitioner relationship. Literature suggests that much of this friction stems from the high emotions involved when children and families are struggling with a need beyond the parameters of that generally considered 'the norm' (Wolfendale, 2013). Orphan (2004, p. 98) explains the emotional impact of this situation:

> Children have a habit of making you aware of feelings inside yourself that you had no idea existed, such as uncontrollable rage, sorrow or a deep sense of joy. This is true for all parents. For parents of children with disabilities the feelings we experience are even more intense and can be fairly constant.

Admittedly the picture of parent partnership painted above, is, overall, rather negative, an image of high pressure and accountability combined with expectations of parents' meek compliance. However, through my own research, I have gained insights into a range of sensitive and multifaceted approaches to working with parents in ECEC settings. In research carried out with EC leaders and practitioners (Solvason, Webb and Sutton-Tsang, 2020a, 2020b; Solvason and Proctor, 2021) evidence emerged of professionals who listened and empathised with parents, who put families' wellbeing before assessment results and, on a daily basis undertook hundreds of small acts of kindness and consideration towards the parents with whom they showed human connectedness.

As is discussed in the Introduction, data collected through TACTYC-funded research suggests that maintained nursery school (MNS) practitioners are adept at building relationships with parents in even the most fraught of circumstances. In addition to these findings, data examined by Solvason and Proctor (2021) suggest that for ECPs, relationships with parents are about far more than compliance. The practitioners that we encountered during our research did not have a myopic aim to produce 'the best assessments results'; instead their goal was to maximise the wellbeing of both parent and child. The data below proposes that the parent–practitioner relationship is a key facet of the holistic empathy and care that ECPs demonstrate towards children and families with whom they work on a daily basis.

A brief overview of research approaches

Data presented in this chapter emerges from surveys and interviews carried out with 115 Maintained Nursery School leaders and practitioners across the Midlands and the Southwest of England. The SEND research (Solvason and Proctor, 2021), on the other hand, was extremely small-scale. The impetus for this emerged from the TACTYC research, posing the question of whether the same approaches to productive relationships were implemented with parents of SEND children, or whether the specificity of some SEND provision and approaches produced 'different' parent–practitioner relationships. After all, 'the life and educational experiences of children with SEND are substantially less positive than those of other children' (Truss, 2008, p. 366) bringing a whole new range of complications. This SEND element of research was of personal interest to both researchers, as parents, relatives and friends of children with SEND.

The SEND research was carried out in partnership with the EC lead for early years at a specialist school. The involvement of this researcher enabled access to the group of specialist teachers with whom he worked. He collected data through one focus group discussion with three teaching colleagues and this process, led by someone already known to the practitioners, enabled openness and confidence that might not have been obtained otherwise (Brink, 1993). The data, obtained through a socially constructed approach, are extremely rich, and provide some insight into the experience and perspective of practitioners. In both research encounters, the aim was to gain insights into, and understanding of, the encounters of those who are living them through a focus upon qualitative data (Denzin and Lincoln, 2013). Both studies adhere to the concept of research 'with' and not 'on' participants (James, 2004) in terms of treating research participants with respect and choice regarding their involvement. Our aim was that both the process and the product of the research should 'bring about good' (Bloor, 2010) in addition to compliance to ethical guidelines (in this case BERA, 2018).

Data analysis

For the purposes of this chapter, I look across both data sources and identify universal themes most pertinent to parent–practitioner partnerships across the range of ECEC settings. All data are anonymised; therefore, only delineated by the use of maintained nursery school practitioner (MNSP) or specialist school practitioner (SSP). Key themes arising across both data sets were: recognising the parent as the expert on their child and the moderator of the child's wellbeing; the importance of empathy; building trust; listening; being kind, and keeping the child in mind. The words of our participants are presented in italics in order to be clearly identifiable.

Parent as expert and moderator of the child's wellbeing

Data from both nursery and special school practitioners suggested they had a strong sense that when they took on a child they would also be working closely with the child's family. This meant that developing positive relationships with key family members was central to that child being adequately supported. As one MNSP said, '*To understand who the child is in front of us, we need to understand their families*'. SSPs, particularly, recognised the expertise of the parent in helping them to understand the child's complex needs. They variously explained it this way:

> There's just so much information and sometimes the parent is the best one, because they've got it all in their heads, they've got the whole life there.
>
> … we need the context of, how their weekend was, how they were this morning, things that might potentially be problematic during the day that we need to be aware of. It's just important to get the whole, wider picture, otherwise we're guessing all day. If the family can just tell us 'oh this can be because of … x,y,z' then it stops us from trying to guess.
>
> If we're ever in doubt I always ask them … and then they kind of trust us, because they know that if there's ever an issue, we'll just check, and we won't kind of, you know, muddle through it. We'll check and make sure that we're doing it properly…

The MNSs practitioners were acutely aware that the more settled the family home, the more children would be '*of a mindset to fully access everything*' in terms of their learning. The data suggest that they felt opportunities for the child were moderated by the wellbeing of the parent. Practitioners recognised that the multiple disadvantages of the families they were working with caused high anxiety, and that by providing support to parents for their needs, they were enabling the children to '*continue to learn*'. As one Maintained Nursery School Practitioner (MNSP) commented: '*you're a place that is there to support their children and to join them in supporting their children*'. Similarly, a Special School Practitioner (SSP) commented that parents '*need support as well, in order to … parent their children in the best way*'.

Practitioners expressed awareness that the child would 'tune into' the relationship that existed between the parents and themselves and react to this. One SSP explained the care with which a parent–practitioner relationship was established and why this was so important:

> … probably the most important part of our job, certainly in early years, because unless you have happy parents, they don't want to leave their children with you … and children pick up on whether their parents are comfortable with you as adults as well.

Similarly, one MNSP specifically referred to the longer-term positive impacts of '*having a really strong relationship with parents*' and how '*it might turn their [the parent's] view around of education and that, in turn, will have a positive impact on the child*'.

Empathy

A specific ECP skill that the data highlighted was the ability of practitioners to *empathise* with parents. (This is discussed in more detail in the chapter that follows.) Data pointed to the way that practitioners sought to understand challenges parents faced rather than judge them for the actions that occurred as a result. Manifestations of empathy in the MNSs were wide-ranging, from being flexible about collection times for a parent with multiple appointments, reassuring the parent that *'he's going to be well cared for and looked after if you're late'*; to providing a temporary, emergency place for a child whose mother might otherwise lose her job. On other occasions it was simply a case of being available, as this MNSP shared:

> We see some families go through some really terrible times. But we were there along the way. And it might have just been a smile in the morning or a hug in the afternoon. A 'Come on, let's go and get a cup of tea'.

SSPs similarly demonstrated a depth of care and concern for parents that they worked with, and an understanding of the very difficult journey that parents will have lived through before arriving at their school doors. As one SSP shared: *'if they've had a bad experience of ... maybe being told very negative things every single day'* it was important that they should introduce positivity about their child's behaviour and say *"look, that's fine... we're fine with that"... just put their minds at rest'*. Similarly, another SSP explained how it was typical, as a parent of a child with SEND to not *'get any contact [from a practitioner] unless there is something negative, and then you get the walk of shame'*. Therefore, they understood parents' defensiveness in their initial communication and that it could take a while for some parents to *'get their heads around that when you're ringing them, it's not always a bad thing'*.

The SSPs described how they needed to tread very gently with parents and *'hold their hand'* when they first arrived because the special school could *'feel like a scary place.'* This SSP explained:

> ...they've had such horrific experiences. But there's an awful lot of just gently coaxing parents at that point, because they have lost trust in all the adults that have been involved in their child's life so far, and they feel deskilled as parents.

SSPs understood that because of the various vulnerabilities of the children with SEND, parents could be *'terrified of leaving them'*. Another reiterated that to the parents, their children were *'very vulnerable and very precious'* and that parents needed *'lots of reassurance'* even if they chose that particular school for their child. As this SSP explains:

> And even those parents who are fighting for their children to come here because they know that's what's right, that's not what they wanted for their child, way back when they first found out they were having that child. They

wanted the, inverted commas, normal life for them. This is, this is blown their lives apart.

The SSPs were sensitive to the fact that even for those families that really *wanted* their child to attend their special school, their lives would never be the same as those families who were not coping with such complicated needs.

Building trust

One MNSP asked rhetorically, *'Good relationships are central to all of it aren't they?'*. So, what did the data reveal about how skilled practitioners went about this? A central facet that emerged was the importance accorded to building trust. As one MNSP stressed: *'I think it's about your reliability. Yeah, I think you have to be utterly reliable to exactly what you're going to do, and you always do it consistently'*. This was reiterated by an SSP who shared that by ensuring dependability, parents' anxiety could be reduced. That they would *'start to realise, this person isn't lying to me! They are actually doing what they said they were going to do … you did what you said you were going to do and they know it's going to happen'*.

A cornerstone of forming trust appeared to be ideas of openness and honesty. The couching of honesty in ways that were not *'brutal'* (SSP) was mentioned as particularly important for those working with families with a child with SEND. This SSP explained, it is about *'honesty and kindness and finding a balance between'*. One SSP specified that for them it was about sharing things with parents as opposed to *'teaching'* them. Practitioners highlighted the importance of respect. For example, this SSP described asking parents *'are you happy with how we've dealt with that? Is there anything you'd like us to do differently?'* to reinforce their regard for the parent, and the idea of an ongoing dialogue. This was also mentioned by the MNSP who described her setting as a *'a predictable, helpful, supportive and non-judgemental community'* for their parents.

This SSP shared the gentleness and positivity with which problems were broached, explaining that honesty was:

> combined with having built a good relationship with them, so that you have that kind of opportunity to be able to say… you know … 'we had a really bad day today… This happened, but its ok because we can move on with it'.

Listening

The importance of listening was mentioned repeatedly, throughout both data sets. This MNSP emphasized the importance of this:

> Parents need to know that if they come here to ask for support, actually, they will be listened to. And it doesn't matter if it's a busy day or not a busy day, you never don't respond, you never don't hear.

The same practitioner went on to state that if a parent felt rebuffed, on just one occasion, the relationship with the setting could potentially be destroyed. Similarly, another MNSP mentioned: '*they just want someone that will listen to them; that will take them seriously, rather than just being fobbed off*'.

A SSP shared:

> I always try and … make sure that …they are aware that we are always here. And if this, you know, becomes a problem … sometimes I might say, you know, 'if you are ever worried, or if you ever do want to talk about something, you know, we are here, to help you?'

Practitioners accepted that they could sometimes be on the receiving end of an angry onslaught from a parent, but the data suggested that they did not take this personally or become affronted. A SSP referred to '*just listening to them when they have to rant*'. Similarly, a MNSP shared:

> I mean, don't get me wrong. We get shouted out, we get sworn at. We are just real with them. I say to them, come on, you're obviously very angry. But I don't think we need to be like this. Come on, let's calm down and sort it out.

Data revealed that all practitioners recognised how vital it was that they were accessible to parents and able to lend a listening ear. This MNSP described how the families they worked with felt about the support that they received from the setting, sharing that they would say: '*I know I'll be listened to. I know somebody will help me here*'.

Keeping the child in mind

One MNSP stressed that always being available to parents was not a case of just '*being nice*' to them, but was about making the needs of the child a priority. She explained: '*We actively demonstrate and model the kind of non-negotiable of holding the needs of children in mind. Yes, that is the thing that we will not negotiate on*'. Put even more simply, this SSP stressed: '*It's not about us! It's about this little person, and that life*'.

An aspect of prioritising the child that came through in discussion with SSPs was the importance of keeping the child safe. As these two practitioners discussed:

> SSP 1: And from a safeguarding point of view as well, we are there to keep them safe and if we don't have the ability to call [the parents] … To be professionally curious, then you can't… fully, you have to be able to …
>
> SSP 2: Yeah, you can't fully safeguard people.

A MNSP explained that genuine concern which focused on the specificity of a child and family's needs could open channels of communication that presented opportunities for support. She said: '*If they can see that you do genuinely care about them and their child, then they do tend to tell you things*'.

Being Kind

The other characteristic of ECP expertise that shone through the data was the significance of an ECP's capacity to demonstrate kindness. So many comments made by SSPs related to acts of kindness carried out to help atone for awful experiences that parents had endured before reaching their setting. One SSP described it this way:

> So … they must be in a very terrible place when they come to us … in that situation often parents can present in a quite a difficult way to us … here. They can be very, very defensive, quite angry sometimes, very frustrated. You just have to remember all that rubbish that they've been through, and be kind to them…

Therefore, the SSPs endeavoured to bring small moments of joy to the parents with tiny acts filled with thoughtfulness, exemplified through the comments below:

> They [the parents] get told a lot they [the child] can't do this and they can't do that … Yeah, they'll never do this, and … just to turn it round and say 'oh, they did this today! It was really good, it was, you know, they were amazing, they … tried so hard!' …

> *SSP 1: They want to know if they're happy…*
> *SSP 2: … you know, all those really important things …*
> *SSP 1: They like to have little anecdotes about them…*
> *SSP 3: … 'did you see that we did this?'*
> *SSP 1: … yeah. 'Look at this they did!'*
> *SSP 2: They want to celebrate them!*

The SSPs endeavoured to provide reassurance and opportunities for parents to experience joyful moments of dialogue about the child. Giving parents this sort of encouraging information meant that they were '*allowed to look at their child in a different way. They're allowed to see them for … the individual that they are*'. Another added, '*they're allowed to enjoy them*'. Two SSPs mentioned parents crying with joy when receiving positive feedback about their child for the first time.

Similarly, MNS practitioners allude to numerous practical acts of kindness for disadvantaged parents which went above and beyond statutory requirements. These extended from help with the paperwork for legal processes to information about accessing food banks and mental health support. But they also recognised the healing power of kind words. As this MNS explained:

> It wasn't just giving that child a nursery place, it never can be … it's that five minutes in the morning, that smile on the door, that when that mom's in a

ratty mood, or the dad, and I say 'oooh, he's been ever so good today, he's done this this and this'. Sometimes I make it up, because I can see the change. Because everyone loves their kid really. Really. To hear something positive … And we can … it's easy to say something positive, isn't it?

Discussion and conclusions

The literature section of this chapter highlights research that details the value to children of a focus on parent partnerships in EC practice. What these texts fail to recognise is the emotional labour central to these relationships (Solvason, Hodgkins, and Watson, 2021), or what a rocky terrain this can be to traverse. As Orphan (2004) explains, the responsibility of being a parent heightens emotions, and makes parents vulnerable in ways that can cause friction with practitioners and other public sector professionals. Statutory and non-statutory duties placed upon those who care for children and families rarely capture the demanding quality of this for both the family and the ECP. An authentic understanding of this dynamic demand lies at the forefront of the ECP's cache of skills.

The data outlined above creates a picture of an ECP who can tune into the socio-emotional needs of parents. This practitioner recognises the parent as expert in knowing the needs of their child and as the chief influence upon the child's emotional wellbeing; a practitioner who is aware of the emotive challenges of parenting, particularly in times of adversity, and prioritises these values over measures of 'cognitive attainment' (Siraj-Blatchford et al., 2002, p. 101). This is a practitioner who seeks to build solid parent partnerships, developed upon respect and trust, rather than the language of antagonism which peppered the findings of Hess, Molina and Kozleski (2006). This is a practitioner who understands that there is a time to talk, but more importantly to *listen* if the needs of the family are to be fully understood. This is a practitioner who keeps the child as the focus for all that they do and strives to celebrate as many precious moments as they are able with their families. As is so often the case, this emotionally demanding aspect of the ECP's complex and highly skilled role frequently goes unrecognised, as ECPs continue to be positioned as 'less than' (Nutbrown, 2013) their counterparts in other phases of the school system.

REFLECTIVE POINTS

Within your own setting:

- To what extent is the holistic wellbeing of the child within the family considered?
- How well do you know the individual circumstances of your families?
- To what extent are the views of parents sought out and valued? (Even those that may be more challenging?) How do you show that you *listen*?
- What do you (explicitly or implicitly) present as the model of the 'good parent'?

References

Alexander, E. 2009. *Understanding Quality and Success in Early Years Settings: Practitioners' Perspectives*. Swindon: ESRC

Ball, S. (1990). *Markets, Morality and Equality in Education*. London: The Tufnell Press.

Baquedano-Lopez, P., Alexander, R. A., and Hernandez, S. J. (2013). Equity issues in parental and commu- nity involvement in schools: What teacher educators need to know. *Review of Research in Education*, 37(1): 149–182.

Bloor, Michael. (2010). The Researcher's Obligation to bring about Good. *Qualitative Social Work*, 9: 17–20. doi:10.1177/1473325009355616

Brink, H. I. L. (1993). Validity and reliability in qualitative research. *Curationis*, 16(2): 35–38. doi:10.4102/curationis.v16i2.1396

British Educational Research Association. (2018). Ethical guidelines for educational research. 4th edn. Available at: https://www.bera.ac.uk/researchers-resources/publications/ethical-guidelines-for-educational-research-2018 (Accessed 17.05.2021).

Broomhead, K. (2013). Blame, Guilt and the Need for 'Labels': Insights from Parents of Children with Special Educational Needs and Educational Teachers. *British Journal of Special Education*, 40(1): 14–21. doi:10.1111/1467-8578.12012

Callanan, M., Anderson, M., Haywood, S., Hudson, R., and Speight, S. (2017). *Study of Early Education and Development (SEED): Good Practice in Early Education Research Report*. Retrieved from: https://assets.publishing.service.gov.uk/government/uploads/system/uploads/attachment_data/file/586242/SEED__Good_Practice_in_Early_Education_-_RR553.pdf

Central Advisory Council for Education. (1967). *The Plowden Report, Children and their Primary Schools*. London: HMSO.

Denzin, N. K., and Lincoln, Y. S. (2013). *The Landscape of Qualitative Research* (4th ed). London: SAGE.

Department for Education. (2004). *Every Child Matters*. London: The Stationery Office.

Department for Education. (2017). *Statutory Framework for the Early Years Foundation Stage*. DfE. https://www.gov.uk/government/publications/early-years-foundation-stage-framework--2 (Accessed 26.03.2020).

Desforges, C., and Abouchaar. A. (2003). *The Impact of Parental Involvement, Parental Support and Family Education on Pupil Achievements and Adjustment: A Literature Review*. Department for Education and Skills. https://dera.ioe.ac.uk/6305/

Early Education.2015. Maintained nursery schools: the state of play report. https://www.early-education.org.uk/sites/default/files/Nursery%20Schools%20State%20of%20Play%20Report%20final%20print.pdf (Accessed 12. 11. 2018).

Haines Lyon, C. (2018). Democratic parent engagement: Relational and dissensual. *Power and Education*, 10(2): 195–208. doi:10.1177/1757743818756913

Hartas, D. (2008). Practices of parental participation: A case study. *Educational Psychology in Practice*, 24(2): 139–153. doi:10.1080/02667360802019206

Henricson, C. (2003). *Government and Parenting: Is There a Case for a Policy Review and a Parents' Code?* The Joseph Rowntree Foundation. https://www.jrf.org.uk/report/resolving-tensions-parenting-policy

Hess, R. S., Molina, A. M. & Kozleski, E. B. (2006). Until Somebody Hears Me: Parent Voice and Advocacy in Special Educational Decision Making. *British Journal of Special Education*, 33(3): 148–157. doi:10.1111/j.1467-8578.2006.00430.x

James, D. (2004). *Research in Practice: Experiences, Insights and Interventions*. From the project Transforming Learning Cultures in Further Education. London: Learning and Skills Development Agency.

Lewis, J., and West, A. (2013). Early childhood education and care in England under Austerity: Continuity or change in political ideas, policy goals, availability, affordability and quality in a childcare market? *Journal of Social Policy*, 46(2): 331–348. doi:10.1017/S0047279416000647

National Council for Curriculum and Assessment. (2009). *Aistear* https://curriculumonline.ie/getmedia/484bcc30-28cf-4b24-90c8-502a868bb53a/Aistear-Principles-and-Themes_EN.pdf

Nutbrown, C. (2013). *Shaking the Foundations of Quality? Why 'childcare' policy must not lead to poor-quality early education and care*. http://www.crec.co.uk/docs/Shaking_the_foundations_of_quality.pdf

Orphan, A. (2004). *Moving On: Supporting Parents of Children with SEND*. London: Fulton.

Ramaekers, S., and Suissa, J. (2011). Parents as 'educators': languages of education, pedagogy and 'parenting'. *Ethics and Education*, 6(2): 197–212.

Reynolds, A. D., Crea, T. M., Medina, J., Degnan, E., and McRoy, R. (2015). A mixed-methods case study of parent involvement in an urban high school serving minority students. *Urban Education*, 50(6): 750–775. doi:10.1177%2F0042085914534272

Sellgren, K. (2020). *Coronavirus: Home-schooling Has Been Hell, Say Parents*. BBC News: https://www.bbc.co.uk/news/education-53319615

Siraj-Blatchford, I., Sylva, K., Muttock, S., Gilden, R., and Bell, D. (2002). *Researching Effective Pedagogy in the Early Years*. London: DfES. DfES research report 356.

Solvason, C., Cliffe, J., and Bailey, E. (2019). Breaking the silence: Providing authentic opportunities for parents to be heard. *Power and Education*, 11(2): 191–203. doi:10.1177/1757743819837659

Solvason, C., Hodgkins, A., and Watson N. (2021). Preparing students for the 'emotion work' of early years practice. *NZ International Research in Early Childhood Education Journal*, 23(1): 14–23.

Solvason, C., and Proctor, S. (2021). 'You have to find the right words to be honest': Nurturing relationships between teachers and parents of children with Special Educational Needs. *Support for Learning*, 36(3): 470–485.

Solvason, C., Webb, R., and Sutton-Tsang, S. (2020a). What is left…? The implications of losing maintained nursery schools for vulnerable children and families in England. *Children and Society*. https://authorservices.wiley.com/api/pdf/fullArticle/16752045

Solvason, C., Webb, R., and Sutton-Tsang, S. (2020b). *Evidencing the Effects of Maintained Nursery Schools' Roles in Early Years Sector Improvements*. Available at https://tactyc.org.uk/research/

Sylva, K., Melhuish, E., Sammons, P., Siraj-Blatchford, I., and Taggart, B. (2004). *The Effective Provision of Pre-school Education (EPPE) Project: Effective Pre-School Education: A longitudinal study funded by the DfES 1997–2004*. Annesley: DfES Publications.

The Scottish Government. (2009). *The Early Years Framework*. https://www.gov.scot/publications/early-years-framework/pages/1/ (accessed 27.03.20).

Truss, C. (2008). Peter's story: Reconceptualising the UK SEND system. *European Journal of Special Needs Education*, 23(4): 365–377. doi:10.1080/08856250802387349

Vygotsky, L. S. (1978). *Mind in Society: The Development of Higher Psychological Processes*. Cambridge, MA: Harvard University Press.

Welsh Government. (2015) *Well-Being of Future Generations (Wales) Act 2015*. https://gweddill.gov.wales/topics/people-and-communities/people/future-generations-act/?lang=en (Accessed 27.03.2020).

Wolfendale, S. (2013). *Working with parents of children with SEN after the Code of Practice*. Hoboken: Taylor and Francis.

4

APPRECIATING AND PRACTISING EMPATHY

Angela Hodgkins

Introduction

Empathy is the ability to understand the feelings of others, to see things through their eyes, to imagine what it would be like to be them in a particular situation (Rogers, 2004). Anyone working with people, especially with young children, should have excellent empathy skills (Boyer, 2010). This chapter explores how Early Childhood Practitioners (ECPs) demonstrate empathy within everyday practice and the impact of this on them. Using empirical data I examine some of the empathy approaches employed by practitioners, along with the rewards and emotional costs.

Defining empathy

One challenge in researching 'empathy' is a lack of a common definition of what it is and how it relates to or differs from sympathy or mimicry. One of the most prolific writers on the subject, Hoffman (2012, p. 30), declares 'the more I study empathy, the more complex it becomes'. Carl Rogers (1942), the name most synonymous with empathy, explored the concept as one of three 'core conditions', along with 'congruence' and 'unconditional positive regard' attributes, he deemed essential in establishing therapeutic relationships. Rogers (2004) had a strong conviction that, they are equally important in all interpersonal relationships. Indeed, Ratka (2018, p. 1140) refers to empathy as 'the most important human attribute that matters in every aspect of life'.

There are different levels of empathy (Belzung, 2014) ranging from primitive at its most basic (for example, yawning when other people yawn) to cognitive which involves reasoning how another person might be feeling. Advanced empathy is a skill that goes further; it involves identifying and 'offering back unstated feelings picked up from body language or voice tone and becoming aware of feelings that

DOI: 10.4324/9781003206262-5

are deeply buried in the other person's subconscious' (Prowle and Hodgkins, 2020, p. 3). For the ECP, advanced empathy could be shown by having an awareness of feelings that children are not yet able to understand or articulate for themselves. In a relationship between a keyworker and child, the ECP *tunes into* the world of the child. This ability to empathically *tune into* others is crucial in developing relationships with children and is also beneficial when working with families and colleagues. In Early Childhood Education and Care (ECEC) management, too, empathy is recognised as a strong characteristic of leadership (Watzlaf, 2019).

Advanced empathy skills

In agreeing that ECPs should demonstrate empathy (Boyer, 2010), what does it mean to be consistently empathic? Recent evidence gathered from a group of ECPs (Hodgkins, 2019) corroborates that practitioners use advanced empathy in their everyday practice, tuning into the child, sensing emotion, using intuition and sensitivity.

FIGURE 4.1 Examples of advanced empathy (from Hodgkins, 2019).

Page and Elfer (2013) also highlight the intuition of practitioners working with very young children. Understanding advanced empathy as an *unconscious way of knowing* is useful: it describes implicitly knowing what to do in a particular situation through drawing on experience. Interest in advanced empathy arose from my own observation of practices in ECEC settings that I was keen to explore further. The research (Hodgkins, 2019) which ensued focussed on experiences of using empathy in EC practice. It was carried out with ECPs who were undertaking a 'Top Up' degree whilst in full time, paid employment in the EC sector. Because of the sensitivity of researching with my own students, it was important to obtain ethical approval and to recognise and negate potential power imbalances. The research aimed to identify examples of advanced empathy within the ECP role and to gather practitioners' views on what was at stake for them emotionally. This qualitative study comprised an anonymous online questionnaire and a small focus group of participants expressed interest. A total of 54 participants completed the questionnaire and 5 of these took part in the focus group.

Research findings demonstrated participants' belief in the importance of empathy, with 86% of respondents viewing empathy as essential in the role, and the other 14% stating that it was important. Participants reported being 'extremely sensitive' to the needs of children and needing 'endless patience' (Hodgkins, 2019, p. 50). The research identified the sensing of emotion as synonymous with advanced empathy, as in this example:

> Knowing the children I work with gives me an insight into their emotional wellbeing. I am aware of slight changes in the way they behave or engage and I usually pick up on it very quickly.

Other participants said, '*This is often done without thought – my actions just naturally mean I have an awareness for these signs*' and '*I know when a child isn't feeling themselves when I first look at them in the morning*'. These examples echo Page and Elfer's (2013) research, which analysed relationships between practitioners and very young children and found evidence of close interactions that place significant emotional demands on them. Page builds on Noddings' (2013) *ethic of care*, using the term 'professional love' (Page, 2018, p. 125) to illustrate particular emotional practices such as intuition, attachment, emotional intimacy and empathy. Practices identified by Page (2018) and Page and Elfer (2013) include many examples of warmth and empathy during physical care routines with young children, including nappy changing and sharing mealtimes. This was echoed in my research, which showed practitioners tuning into children during routine activities such as tidy up time and during arrivals and departures from nursery. Egan (2013) discusses how noticing, and interpreting children's body language, is an important aspect of advanced empathy that can help ECPs to pre-empt difficulties. This appeared to be the case in the examples from my own data illustrated in Figure 4.1.

In order to identify subtle emotional signs in the children, ECPs need to be vigilant, perceptive and sensitive. Many examples described in studies by Page and Elfer (2013) and Hodgkins (2019) demonstrate strong emotions in children, and subsequently in the practitioners who care for or even *love* (Page, 2018) them. Page and Elfer's study (2013, p. 560) highlights the 'emotional complexities of managing such close, personal interactions'; Datler et al. (2010, p. 82) concur, accentuating 'how hard and disturbing it is, to be confronted so intimately with the often-catastrophic emotions of very young children'. It is unsurprising, then, that practitioners find themselves personally affected by such strong emotions and demands. The parameters of the ECPs role do not stop with the children; they are also required to call upon empathy skills in interactions with parents, families and colleagues. There is a need to be understanding of challenges experienced by parents (Solvason et al., 2019). Parents' emotional needs can be extreme, and ECPs need to be sensitive towards ensuing behaviours (Solvason and Proctor, 2021), listening, and responding considerately. Page and Elfer's (2013, p. 562) study of attachments in nurseries highlighted many examples of ECPs' 'remarkable capacity to reach out to parents in difficulty'. Solvason et al. (2021, p. 17) suggest that supporting parents is emotionally demanding and that ECPs are often '*assumed to be able to manage this without any recognition of the specific expertise required*'.

Empathy and compassion

The terms *empathy* and *compassion* can be confused and mistakenly used interchangeably (Singer and Klimecki, 2014): however, they are different concepts. Empathy is the capacity to share the feelings of others (Rogers, 1942), and compassion can be one of the consequences resulting *from* empathy. Singer and Klimecki (2014) suggest that two possible reactions to empathy are compassion (which they also term 'empathic concern' or 'sympathy') or empathic distress. Reacting with compassion leads to the motivation to help, whereas empathic distress can result in withdrawal from a situation to protect oneself emotionally (discussed in the next section). Compassion is empathy expressed through action; hence it is possible to have empathy without compassion, feeling the suffering of others without being urged to do anything to alleviate the suffering. Compassion can be thought of as the positive outcome of empathy, with empathic distress being the negative outcome.

ECPs who demonstrate empathy daily within their role should be aware of the impact it may have on them. Although empathy enhances practice, it can also result in feelings of tiredness and the internalising of distress (Tone and Tully, 2014). Elfer (2012) argues that coping mechanisms and supportive supervision are essential to cope with the emotional demands of the ECP role. A participant of the focus group in my own research described a strategy she had developed to cope with the emotional demands (Figure 4.2):

> I have taught myself to express myself and the anxiety and stress that I am feeling. Without this, I feel that I would not cope with the pressures of work and the processing and reflection of my daily working practice.

Empathic distress – the cost of empathy?

Empathic distress is similar to what is commonly known as 'compassion fatigue' (Figley, 2013, pp. 2–3). The close responsive relationships that ECPs form with children and their families can be powerful and intense (Datler et al., 2010), yet there is a lack of recognition of the emotional complexity of the role for practitioners (Page and Elfer, 2013). In recent years, there has been increased interest in researching the emotional demands of ECEC work. Taggart (2016), Elfer (2018), Page (2018), and Hodgkins (2019) have all found compassion *fatigue* within the sector.

Hochschild (2013, p. 50), in her work on the 'commercialization of human feeling' asserts that those working in roles with people are expected to manage or suppress emotions that are seen as inappropriate and to introduce positive emotion

Appreciating and practising empathy 45

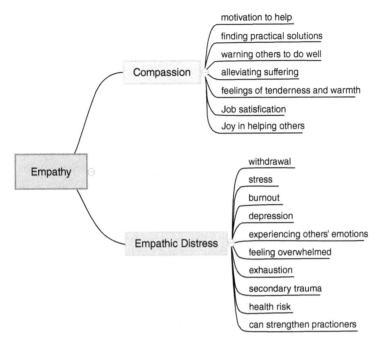

FIGURE 4.2 Empathy resulting in compassion versus empathic distress, based on ideas by Hansen et al. (2018).

cues, or "feeling rules" consistent with the image required for the job. Hochschild (2013, p. 7) defines emotional labour as:

> the management of feeling to create a publicly observable facial and bodily display ... this labour requires one to induce or suppress feelings in order to sustain the outward countenance that produces the proper state of mind in others.

Hochschild's (2013) interpretation of a worker requires demonstration of particular feelings as part of the role. Examples of this for ECPs might be a requirement to have, or at least demonstrate, empathy and 'endless patience' (Elfer, 2012, p. 365). Hochschild (1983, p. 52) proposed that 'to be warm and loving to a child who kicks, screams and insults you ... a child whose problem is unlovability ... requires emotion work'. In some instances, this may be merely 'surface acting', but it is more likely that the emotion which has been worked for and developed, is very real (Hochschild, 1983). Feelings associated with emotional labour can have personal consequences for the ECP. There have been many studies on the negative effects of emotional labour (Hochschild, 1983, 2013) and the stress that can result from it, arising from the coordination of mind and feelings, which Hochschild (2013, p. 7) believes 'draws on a source of self that we honour as deep and integral to our own individuality'. Emotional stress, which is *not* dealt with can develop into burnout, a condition where a person can no longer manage their emotions and becomes emotionally exhausted with a perceived lack of personal accomplishment (Maslach, Jackson and Leiter, 1997). There is evidence to suggest that 'surface acting' leads to more exhaustion and more absenteeism than 'deep acting' (Kammeyer-Mueller et al., 2013). Hochschild (1983) describes 'surface acting', for example, putting on a fake smile, whereas deep acting involves making an effort to feel the emotions of others. Deep acting is synonymous with empathy; being sensitive to, and tuning into, the child so that we can feel the emotions ourselves as practitioners. Tone and Tully (2014) identify empathy as a particularly 'risky strength' when developing and working with emotion. It involves internalising others' pain, comes with the risk of personal distress for some vulnerable to depression and anxiety. My research with ECPs (Hodgkins, 2019) highlighted examples of negative effects of empathy within Early Years practice contexts (Figure 4.3).

A study by Zahn-Waxler and Van Hulle (2012) suggests that empathy can interfere with social and emotional development and can lead to feelings of guilt, when we are unable to make a difference to others. This guilt, they add, can consequently lead to depression. Working with others who are in distress and in need of comfort is a necessary part of the role of the ECP, but individuals cope with this in different ways. Tone and Tully (2014) suggest that individuals who demonstrate empathy but do not have well-established coping skills will ruminate on their role in stressful situations and focus on comforting themselves, thus exacerbating feelings of stress, hence empathy is 'a risky strength'. This demonstrates a clear need for emotional support for ECPs, allowing practitioners to talk through feelings and identify coping mechanisms and sources of support (Hodgkins, 2021).

The Early Childhood workforce is diverse, with practitioners coming from myriad backgrounds with a range of qualifications. This can cause conflict or stress.

> If there's been a difficult issue, I dwell on it if a child has been upset. Sometimes my 'patience bucket' has been well and truly drained at work and this can make me short with my own children – not something to be proud about.

> I just observe all emotion and absorb all emotions and so if I'm with somebody that's very negative, I am automatically in a bad mood. I find it hard to come out of that

> Having recently been diagnosed with work stress, I can relate to how work impacts on our personal lives. When work is always on my mind, it's difficult to make space for other things and this leads to me feeling resentful of my job.

FIGURE 4.3 Examples of negative effects of emotional labour (from Hodgkins, 2019).

ECPs are expected to work harmoniously with a range of colleagues, families and other professionals; consequently, practitioners may also experience having to strive to 'submerge conflict arising from diverse cultural values and expectations regarding close relationships with children, different trainings and different conditions of service' (Elfer, 2012, p. 130). This emotional labour is often unacknowledged and undervalued. My research with ECPs revealed that stress is a feature of the profession for majority of practitioners.

Effective supervision, therefore, becomes essential for ECPs to talk through feelings and to manage increasingly complex and demanding roles (Elfer, 2012; Tone and Tully, 2014); however, my research found that this can be variable in terms of the quality and effectiveness of support offered to individuals.

Empathy and job satisfaction

Although much is written about compassion fatigue in caring occupations, it is important to remember that there is also considerable 'compassion satisfaction' too, and even evidence that the more we empathise, the more satisfaction we feel. It is possible, then, that the positive consequences of feeling empathy can compensate for its negative other. Studies have shown that exposure to those in need can generate a positive self-image and stronger appreciation of different values in life (Jeon and Wells, 2018; Kim and Yang, 2016). Research by Inegaki and Orehek (2017) suggests that doing things for others, nurturing and supporting, results in positive feelings of self-esteem, self-worth and social connection. Harr and Moore (2011) claim that compassion satisfaction can improve the mental, physical and spiritual well-being of all helping professionals. They maintain that it may also be a motivator and could help 'mitigate the negative effects of burnout and compassion fatigue' (ibid.). Peck et al.'s (2015) research into preschool teachers in the United States proposes that helping practitioners to develop empathy skills during training or at the beginning of their careers could help to increase job satisfaction and result in teachers remaining in the profession for longer. There appears to be a need for this: in the UK today, the ECEC profession is unstable, with one in six ECPs leaving within a year (Burns, 2020). A similar situation is occurring in Australia (Jackson, 2021) and the USA (Basloe, 2020) with two out of three ECPs leaving. In each case, the reasons given for leaving ECEC are related to low pay, lack of appreciation and lack of support for the emotional labour involved. Research carried out by the Anna Freud Centre (Nelinger et al., 2021) detailed difficulties experienced by ECPs during the worldwide COVID-19 pandemic.

The report identified 71% of ECPs had been stressed or upset when dealing with difficult situations (ibid., p. 2). However, Ortlepp and Friedman (2002) suggest that this may not always be negative, as working with intense or traumatic situations can lead to some positive changes in personal maturity as well as a deeper understanding of other people. Research by Hesse (2002) similarly indicates that emotionally demanding work provides people with an opportunity to develop on both personal and professional levels. Perhaps this is one reason many continue to work in ECECs, despite evidence of the negative consequences that may arise.

Empathy – the gender issue

The vast majority of practitioners working with young children in the UK are female; this is even more pronounced in the ECEC sector, where 98% of workers identify as women (Hemmings, 2018). This becomes significant in a consideration of just who is regarded as the *right* kind of person to work with young children. The list of attributes includes: being caring (Noddings, 1984), loving (Cousins, 2017) and having emotional warmth (Cameron and Maginn, 2008). Soft skills such as empathy and compassion are still habitually considered to be feminine traits (Osgood, 2010).

ECPs regularly prioritise children's emotions above their own (Solvason et al., 2021). The regulation of emotions could be due to an assumption that in a female-dominated workforce, women are 'better biologically equipped to demonstrate altruism and self-sacrifice' (Jovanovic, 2013, p. 529). As careers involving emotional labour comprise over half of the jobs that women undertake, and merely a quarter of traditional male employment (Hochschild, 2013), the management of feelings becomes seen as integral to women's roles.

However, through a critical and feminist lens, attributes of caring are no longer presumed to be the preserve of only women. Rather, empathy is 'mutual, interactive, and humanist' (Freedburg and Gallese, 2007, p. 198). This means be alert to using language which deploys empathy as a *human* characteristic or disposition forming part of a responsive, respectful, and empowering relationship, regardless of sex and gender, encapsulating empathy, communication and teamwork. An experiment by Baez et al. (2017) found no tangible difference in empathy demonstrated by males and females, although there was a difference in self-reporting of the significance of empathy. Women portrayed themselves as being more empathic, suggesting that their responses are influenced by their own identifications and ideas of gender norms.

Celebrating practitioner empathy

Empathy is recognised within ECEC as a crucial characteristic within a sector comprising people who care for children with a variety of needs. Children need ECPs to encourage and empower them, to help them to focus, to uncover and nurture talents, to guide and protect them. As Taggart (2013) emphasises, caring for other people's children, 'supporting young human beings with compassion and cultivating a healthy society', is surely one of the most important of roles in humanity. ECPs gain pleasure from their work with young children and know that the connection between a practitioner and child is not one-sided, but reciprocity that is rewarding for both parties. Noddings (2004, p. 51) explains that 'when we care, we are touched by the other and expect to touch him [sic]. We enter into a relation [...], but that relation need not be one of interference or control'. Spending time with children, being mindful, empathic and compassionate is the key to 'heartful practice' (Dachyshyn, 2015, p. 33) and, ultimately, can bring joy to both parties.

Conclusion

This chapter began with an attempt to define empathy, although it is complex with many facets. Whilst many writers have described types and stages of empathy, there is a consensus within the literature that Rogers' (1942) explanation of an ability to understand the world from someone else's viewpoint is one that is readily understandable (Hoffman, 2012). Such an aptitude is highly valuable in a caring profession. Consideration of ECEC practice reveals examples of ECPs demonstrating empathy to understand and *tune into* the worlds of individual children. Examples from the advanced empathy research with ECPs (Hodgkins, 2019) show their ability to understand how a child feels and an awareness of subtle signs indicating the emotional state of the child.

Empathy is a *soft skill* that is routinely seen as a feminine quality (Osgood, 2010), synonymous with nurturing and mothering. In a sector that remains predominantly female, these soft skills are in demand and there may be a presumption that the vocational nature of the work, and the desire to make a difference, is more valuable than monetary reward. The complexity of emotional labour (Hochschild, 2013) makes it difficult to reconcile professionalism with the demonstration of emotion. My own research reveals the effects that this emotional labour can have on the ECP.

Importantly, there is evidence of the positive impact of empathy, demonstrating that it results in improved self-esteem and compassion satisfaction for the practitioner (Hansen et al., 2018). Relationships between ECPs and children are not one-sided, and the evolution of such relationships can be rewarding and joyous. There is a passion within ECEC for building meaningful 'heartful' relationships with children and a devotion to children and their families should be celebrated.

Moving forward, the need for support for practitioners is evident. The emotional demands of the role stem from the maintenance of emotionally close relationships with young children (Elfer, 2012) and interactions with families (Solvason et al., 2021). It appears that, while some practitioners have well-established coping skills, others do not and can suffer considerable stress in response to their empathic interactions (Hodgkins, 2019; Tone and Tully, 2014). Coping skills can be developed by utilising professional reflection in the form of work discussion within ECP teams (Elfer, 2012). This may answer the need for emotional support for practitioners with opportunities to talk through feelings and identify further supportive sources (Hodgkins, 2021). In current times, a lack of appreciation for the inherent emotional labour of the practitioner role seems to have become even more challenging (Nelinger et al., 2021). It is more important than ever to find ways of rectifying this.

> **REFLECTIVE POINTS**
>
> 1. What does empathy mean for you in your own practice?
> 2. Have you experienced empathic distress or burnout? What coping mechanisms have you developed?
> 3. Which aspects of your role provide you with satisfaction and joy?

References

Baez, S., Flichtentrei, D., Prats, M., Mastandueno, R., Gracia, A., Cetkovitch, M. and Ibanez, A. (2017). Men, women … who cares? A population-based study on sex differences and gender roles in empathy and moral cognition, *PLoS ONE*, 12(6), 1–21.

Basloe, M. (2020). *Leaving the Classroom: Lessons from those who have left childcare jobs*, available at https://www.childcareservices.org/2020/03/06/leaving-the-classroom-lessons-from-those-who-have-left-child-care-jobs/ (accessed 18 July 2021).

Belzung, C. (2014). Empathy, *Journal for Perspectives of Economic, Political, and Social Integration*, 19(1–2), 177–191.

Boyer, W. (2010). Empathy development in teacher candidates, *Early Childhood Education Journal*, 38, 313–321.

Burns, J. (2020). *Early-years workers quit 'underpaid and undervalued' jobs*, BBC News, available at https://www.bbc.co.uk/news/education-53649895 (accessed 18 July 2021)

Cameron, R. and Maginn, C. (2008). The authentic warmth dimension of professional childcare, *British Journal of Social Work*, 38, 1151–1172.

Cousins, S. (2017). Practitioners' constructions of love in early childhood education and care, *International Journal or Early Childhood Education*, 25(1), 16–29.

Dachyshyn, D. M. (2015). Being mindful, heartful, and ecological in early years care and education, *Contemporary Issues in Early Childhood*, 16(1), 32–41.

Datler, W., Datler, M. and Funder, A. (2010). Struggling against a feeling of becoming lost: A young boy's painful transition to day care, *Infant Observation*, 13(1), 65–87.

Egan, G. (2013). *The skilled helper, A problem-management and opportunity-development approach to helping* (10th ed.). Mason, OH: Brooks/Cole, Cengage Learning.

Elfer, P. (2012). Emotion in nursery work: Work Discussion as a model of critical professional reflection, *Early Years*, 32(2), 129–141.

Elfer, P., Greenfield, S., Robson, S., Wilson, D. and Zachariou, A. (2018). Love, satisfaction and exhaustion in the nursery: Methodological issues in evaluating, the impact of work discussion groups in the nursery, *Early Child Development and Care*, 188(7), 892–904.

Freedburg, D. and Gallese, V. (2007). Motion, emotion and empathy in esthetic experience, *Trends in Cognitive Science*, 11(5), 197–203.

Hansen, E., Hakansson Eklund, J., Hallen, A., Stockman Bjurhager, C., Norrstrom, E., Viman, A. and Stocks, E., (2018), Does feeling empathy lead to compassion fatigue or compassion satisfaction? The role of time perspective, *The Journal of Psychology*, 152(8), 630–645.

Harr, C. and Moore, B. (2011), Compassion fatigue among social work students in field placements, *Journal of Teaching in Social Work*, 31(3), 350–363.

Hemmings, C. (2018*). Men can be nursery teachers too*, BBC News [online], available at https://www.bbc.co.uk/news/education-43386250, (accessed 25 November 2019).

Hesse, A. (2002). Secondary trauma: How working with trauma survivors helps therapists, *Clinical Social Work Journal*, 30(3), 293–309.

Hochschild, A. (1983). *The managed heart: Commercialization of human feeling*. Berkeley, California: University of California Press.

Hochschild, A. (2013). *The managed heart – Commercialization of human feeling*. Berkeley, California: University of California Press.

Hodgkins, A. (2019). Advanced empathy in the early years – A risky strength? *NZ International Research in Early Childhood Education Journal*, 22(1), 46–58.

Hodgkins, A. (2021). Early years practitioners need emotional support too, *Nursery Management Today*, 21(2), 33.

Hoffman, M. (2012). *Empathy and moral development*. New York: Cambridge University Press.

Inegaki, T. and Orehek, E. (2017). On the Benefits of Giving Social Support: When, Why, and How Support Providers Gain by Caring for Others, *Current Directions in Psychological Science*, 26 (2),109–113.

Jackson, J. (2021). *Early childhood educators are leaving in droves. Here are 3 ways to keep them, and attract more*, available at https://theconversation.com/early-childhood-educators-are-leaving-in-droves-here-are-3-ways-to-keep-them-and-attract-more-153187 (accessed 18 July 2021).

Jeon, L. and Wells, M. (2018). An organizational-level analysis of early childhood teachers' job attitudes: workplace satisfaction affects early head start and head start teacher turnover, *Child and Youth Care Forum*, 47, 563–581.

Jovanovic, J. (2013). Retaining early childcare educators, *Gender, Work and Organisation*, 20 (5), 528–544.

Kammeyer-Mueller, J. D., Rubenstein, A. L., Long, D. M., Odio, M. A., Buckman, B. R., Zhang, Y. and Halvorsen-Ganepola, M. D. K. (2013). A meta-analytic structural model of dispositional affectivity and emotional labor, *Personnel Psychology*, 66, 47–90.

Kim, S. and Yang, S. (2016). Childcare teachers' job satisfaction: Effects of personality, conflict-handling, and organizational characteristics, *Social Behaviour and Personality*, 44(2), 177–184.

Maslach, C., Jackson, S. E. and Leiter, M. P. (1997). Maslach burnout inventory. In C. P. Zalaquett and R. J. Wood (Eds.), *Evaluating stress: A book of resources* (191–218). Lanham, MD: Scarecrow Education.

Nelinger, A., Album, J., Haynes, A. and Rosan, C. (2021). *Their challenges are our challenges*, available at annafreud.org (accessed 11 August 2021).

Noddings, N. (2004) Caring. In: Pinar, W (ed.) *Contemporary Curriculum Discourses: Twenty Years of JCT* (2nd ed.). New York: Counterpoints, 42–55.

Noddings, N. (1984). *Caring, a feminine approach to ethics & moral education*. Berkley, California: University of California Press.

Noddings, N. (2013). *Caring: A relational approach to ethics and moral education* (2nd ed.). University of California Press.

Ortlepp, K. and Friedman, M. (2002). Prevalence and correlates of secondary traumatic stress in workplace lay trauma counsellors, *Journal of Traumatic Stress*, 15(3), 213–222.

Osgood, J. (2010). Reconstructing professionalism in ECEC: The case for the 'critically reflective emotional professional'. *Early Years*, 30(2), 119–133.

Page, J. (2018). Characterising the principles of professional love in early years care and education, *International Journal of Early Years Education*, 26(2), 125–141.

Page, J. and Elfer, P. (2013). The emotional complexity of attachment interactions in nursery, *European Early Childhood Education Research Journal*, 21(4), 553–567.

Peck, N., Maude, S. and Brotherson, M. (2015). Understanding preschool teachers' perspectives on empathy: A qualitative inquiry, *Early Childhood Education Journal*, 43 (3), 169–179.

Prowle, A. and Hodgkins, A. (2020). *Making a difference with children and families: Reimagining the role of the practitioner*. London: Palgrave Macmillan.

Ratka, A. (2018). Empathy and the development of affective skills, *American journal of pharmaceutical education*, 82 (10), 7192.

Rogers, C. (1942). *Counselling and psychotherapy*. Cambridge, MA: Riverside Press.

Rogers, C. (2004). *On becoming a person*, London: Constable.

Singer, T. and Klimecki, O. (2014). Empathy and compassion, *Current Biology*, 24 (18), 875–878.

Solvason, C., Cliffe, J. and Bailey, E. (2019). Breaking the silence: Providing authentic opportunities for parents to be heard, *Power and Education*, 11 (2), 191–203.

Solvason, C., Hodgkins, A. and Watson, N. (2021). Preparing students for the 'emotion work' of early years practice, *NZ International Research in Early Childhood Education Journal*, 23(1), 14–23.

Solvason, C. and Proctor, S. (2021). 'You have to find the right words to be honest': Nurturing relationships between teachers and parents of children with special educational needs, *Support for Learning*, 36(3), 470–485.

Taggart, G. (2013). The importance of empathy, *Nursery World*, 14 May.

Taggart, G. (2016). Compassionate pedagogy: The ethics of care in early childhood professionalism, *European Early Childhood Education Research Journal*, 24(2), 173–185.

Tone, E. and Tully, E. (2014). Empathy as a 'risky strength': A multilevel examination of empathy and risk for internalizing disorders, *Development and Psychopathology, suppl Multilevel Developmental Perspectives Toward Understanding*, 26(4), 1547–1565.

Watzlaf, V. (2019). Soft skills and the importance of empathy in health information management, *Journal of American Health Information Management Association*, 90(5), 7.

Zahn-Waxler, C. and Van Hulle, C. (2012). Empathy, guilt, and depression: When caring for others becomes costly to children. In B. Oakley, A. Knafo, G. Madhavan and D. Wilson (Eds.), *Pathological altruism* (321–344). New York: Oxford University Press.

5
VALUING CHILDREN WITH SPECIAL EDUCATIONAL NEEDS AND DISABILITY

Samantha Sutton-Tsang

Introduction

During the TACTYC commissioned research into the functions of Maintained Nursery Schools (MNSs, Solvason, Webb and Sutton-Tsang, 2020), leaders and practitioners narrated their own, everyday experiences of their role and the ways in which they believed they impacted upon the lives of young children with Special Educational Needs and Disabilities (SEND), and their families. The challenge of SEND was encapsulated by two MNS leaders in the study: one, through her focus on the number of children with different SEND in her own setting – ranging from two-thirds of two-year-olds to one-third of three- and four-year-olds – at any one time, and the other through her exploration of the lack of clarity in the Early Childhood Education and Care (ECEC) sector more generally about who should bear responsibility for SEND. She explained:

> I just think there's a massive inequality issue for preschool age children with special needs. Because it's not compulsory. So settings do not have to have them [children with SEND], we often get children who've been turned away from setting after setting. And then, at some point, somebody says, you know, who'll support you? Our nursery school.

By sharing the 'voices' of leaders and practitioners in MNSs, this chapter positions the Early Childhood Practitioner (ECP) as an expert practitioner, supporting children with SEND, regardless of the challenges within the sector generally, including practitioner's level of remuneration and professional grade or responsibility, as revealed by the data. I begin by contextualising the data and a discussion of this, by locating SEND more broadly within a literature of an evolving awareness and understanding of SEND in education and specifically within ECEC in England.

DOI: 10.4324/9781003206262-6

The evolution of understandings of SEND within education

The idea of an inclusive approach to children with SEND within the mainstream education system is a relatively new phenomenon. It has arisen from societal changes in the late twentieth century concerning people's attitude towards individuals with additional needs and disabilities. This came about through a shift from a broadly Medical Model of Disability to the more widely, and currently, accepted idea of Social Model of Disability (Borkett, 2021). The medical model assumes the individual with the disability has a problem that needs 'fixing', whereas a social model places the onus for change upon institutions within society (see Oliver, 1990). Historically, individual children who required specialist care were often placed in special day schools or sent away to residential institutions (Borkett, 2021). However, following the publication of *The Warnock Report* in 1978, public perception of inclusion shifted and integration of children with specific needs into mainstream schools became key to informing the ensuing formulation and implementation of The Education Act 1981. This act highlighted the responsibility of local authorities for identifying children with SEND and for arranging the necessary assessments and accommodation to take place to best suit their particular needs.

Warnock's (1978) review of education for children with SEND spearheaded changes in terminology, inclusive actions by all concerned and mainstream education entitlement for all. This included support for children in the Early Childhood Education and Care (ECEC) sector with specific SEND issues, or those children who seemed not to be developing at the same rate as their peers (Borkett, 2021). Following Warnock, increasing numbers of parents began opting for their children to be educated in a mainstream setting, rather than in a special school. Although heralded as the epitome of the social model, this has not been seen wholly as an unwarranted success, with some (including Barton, 2005; Frederick, 2005; Hodkinson, 2010) arguing that the universalist application of Warnock's principles has resulted in a disservice to some SEND children whose specific requirements are left uncatered for to the detriment of their shorter- and longer-term education and thriving. Solvason and Proctor (2021) have explored the vastly different experiences of parents with children of statutory school-age with SEND in both mainstream and specialist schools. This research has highlighted some parents' sense of a lack of training, knowledge and experience of SEND of some mainstream teachers, in contrast to the particular knowledge and provision in some specialist settings that are able to involve parents more actively as partners in the children's experiences.

With the introduction of the United Nations Convention on the Rights of the Child (1989) and the Salamanca Statement (UNESCO, 1994), the social model of disability gained further recognition, focusing on the human rights of the parent and child to participate in decision-making as affecting the child with SEND (Department for Education and Department, DfE, of Health, DoH, 2015). The Special Educational Needs and Disability Act 2001 (SENDA) made further changes to the Education Act 1996, which required schools to prepare for and demonstrate strategic planning for children with SEND. This focused on the need for root and branch changes to provision to ensure inclusive approaches to practice for all children, rather than just the accommodation of SEND children into existing mainstream provision and practices. According to Section 25 of the Children and Families Act 2014, local authorities had a duty to ensure integration between education, training, health and social care provision to promote the wellbeing and improve the quality of life for children with SEND, including their experience in educational settings. The concept of inclusion has now become a ubiquitous idea within education where, as Alderson (2018, p. 177) notes, all children should be respected, regardless of their 'special need' with 'each individual having a unique mixture of strengths, limitations and hopes' which can be accommodated and – indeed – celebrated. This ubiquity leads Hodkinson (2010) to therefore question the usefulness of the term 'inclusion' and whether it serves the broad spectrum of sometimes complex and distinctive needs experienced by some children. Despite the focus on inclusion for all children, *The Special Educational Needs and Disability Code of Practice: 0 to 25 years* (DfE and DoH, 2015, pp. 15–16) does distinguish those children with SEND as those having:

> …a disability which prevents or hinders him or her from making use of facilities of a kind generally provided for others of the same age…
>
> For children aged two or more, special educational provision is educational or training provision that is additional to or different from that made generally for other children or young people of the same age

Currently, all ECEC facilities, regardless of type, must have arrangements to support children with SEND. In addition, MNSs and other settings that are funded by the local authority to deliver early education and preschool places must all follow the *Special Educational Needs (SEN) Code of Practice* (DfE and DoH, 2015). It is general expectation that all ECECs offer a range of support for children with additional needs. With the Early Years Foundation Stage (EYFS) (DfE, 2017a), the statutory framework for children from birth to 5 years of age, the standards of care and education are outlined and must be met for all children, including those with additional needs. In addition, all ECEC settings must show that they provide support for children with SEND and must have a clear strategy for that support. *The Early Years: guide to the 0-25 SEND code of practice: Advice for early years providers that are funded by the local authority* (DfE, 2014, p. 9) states why this is crucial:

> The benefits of early identification are widely recognised – identifying need at the earliest point, and then making effective provision, improves long-term outcomes for children … All those who work with young children should be alert to emerging difficulties and respond early.…

This means that the current EYFS framework requires non-maintained providers (those that are private, voluntary or independent) to have arrangements in place for identifying and meeting children's SEND, thereby promoting equality of opportunity for all children. This should form part of the provider's overall approach to monitoring the ongoing assessment of all children's progress and development (DfE, 2017a). Indeed, The Early Years Workforce Strategy (DfE, 2017b, p. 32) states:

> We want all early years staff to feel confident that they can support a child with SEND to access and enjoy their early years setting. It is also important for staff to have the ability to work effectively with other professionals to meet a child's needs and engage parents positively.

So regardless of preschool type – whether maintained or non-maintained – all ECEC settings requires ECPs to have the skills and knowledge to identify young children's emerging difficulties and to be ready to respond to early concerns about developmental delay or specific SEND issues. Any concerns should be shared by practitioners sensitively with parents or carers who are deemed to know their children. This requires ECPs to therefore seek out their knowledge and perspectives and to listen to and respond empathetically to them with a view to working with them for the best possible short- and long-term outcomes for their child.

The maintained nursery school and SEND

MNSs are required to provide an integrated approach to care, education, health and other services for the children and families. They are led by specialist early years head teachers, qualified teachers and practitioners (Early Education, 2015), and they are often located within urban conurbations in areas of social and economic disadvantage. Their remit is focused explicitly on 'closing the gap' between children in their location and groups of wider peers through the quality of the services they provide; the expertise of their practitioners, including the dissemination of ongoing professional development for all ECECs whether in the maintained or non-maintained sector. However, as research has highlighted (Pascal and Bertram, 2019; Solvason, Webb and Sutton-Tsang, 2020), there are both financial and structural threats to the viability of the MNS, which includes their ability to provide outreach and wider support and integrated ways of working with non-maintained ECECs, including in the area of supporting SEND training for practitioners and support for children.

Due to the high number of local authority referrals of children with SEND to MNSs from the wider non-maintained sector, there is often a concentration of specialist practitioner expertise amongst staff which has evolved over the years. Non-maintained ECECs are not duty-bound to take children with complex SEND if they do not feel that they are sufficiently well-equipped for the child (Early Education, 2015, p. 11) to meet the child's particular needs. This means that MNSs often take children with a wide range of SEND and complex needs (Early Education, 2015). In a survey conducted by Early Education (2018) it was reported that MNS staff qualifications were wide-ranging, with many with postgraduate qualifications in autism, medical training and speech and language therapy. The research also highlighted the opportunities for in-house continuing professional development which practitioners took advantage of to enhance their knowledge and understanding. Our own research corroborated these findings, demonstrating that, when asked about their experiences of practice with SEND, MNS practitioners were able to provide many examples of their own knowledge, as well as their sharing of practice with colleagues within their own settings, and more widely with non-maintained ECEC settings, with a view to supporting children with SEND, alongside their families, albeit against a backdrop of increasing constrained resources and local authority funding so to do.

Methodology

The data presented here is part of a wider data set from the original TACTYC research (Solvason, Webb, and Sutton-Tsang, 2020). The project built on previous research (Paull and Popov, 2019; Pascal and Bertram, 2019) with the aim of enhancing knowledge of the role and responsibilities of MNSs within ECEC sector improvements. A case study approach was adopted, with data from two contrasting local authorities, using a mixed methods approach. This involved data provided through telephone and face-to-face interviews, setting visits and focus groups with a range of practitioners of different levels and types of experience. Two hundred MNSs were invited to take part (100 in the Midlands and 100 in the South and South-East of England). There were 60 MNS leader and 55 practitioner survey responses. Themes identified within the survey data were explored further through interviews and setting visits. In the data below, for the purposes of anonymity, quotations are drawn from the original research, but not specifying details of either setting or speaker.

Data and discussion

Our research demonstrated the way in which MNS practitioners and their leaders took their SEND responsibilities very seriously. Their attention to, and knowledge of the links between disadvantage and aspects of SEND, became apparent, as well as their commitment to findings ways to support children with specific needs, even when the resources and the funding were not readily available. They focused on continuing professional development, both their own, and on findings ways to support practitioner colleagues within the non-maintained sector whenever possible. They were attuned to, and focused upon, their capacity to impact not only the child, celebrating difference and diversity and stepping up to the demands presented by a disability that had not previously been encountered within the setting. Despite financial uncertainty and the many challenges of working in areas of poverty and disadvantage, the data from our research provided clear evidence of the positive impact that experienced and knowledgeable ECPs can have on their communities, acting as 'preventative services' with the potential to mitigate against costly services for the setting and families in the future (Solvason, Webb and Sutton-Tsang, 2020). The research insights concurred with those of Pascal and Bertram (2019) who reported the benefits for children and families accessing MNSs, and particularly for those with SEND and from backgrounds of socio-economic disadvantage. The voices of practitioners are easily identifiable as they are presented in italics.

The well-informed and committed MNS practitioner

Many MNS practitioners told us about the *'moral obligation'* that they felt for the wellbeing of all children but especially those with SEND and multiple disadvantages particularly in light of the dramatic reduction of other local authority public services over the ten to fifteen years due to austerity. They saw their remit and value-system as concerned with providing *'front line support'*. As one head teacher explained, *'Our SEND children all deserve one-to-one support to achieve their full potential. We have a duty of care to help them achieve this'*.

Many also saw their role as actively concerned with inclusive curricular development for the sector. Responses to one survey question highlighted that 14% of practitioners and 16% of leaders had been involved in development activities which focused on SEND over the preceding twelve-month period. Considering their own ongoing development needs to become better informed also featured prominently in the data with one leader mentioning the enhanced specialist training that they had received in physical and sensory development recently which had become invaluable for attending to the needs of the children in their setting. Many practitioners saw the challenge of a child with a particular SEND need as an opportunity for the setting to learn from the child, and to improve its provision and expertise more generally, as demonstrated in the account of one head teacher:

> *We had a little boy who was blind, so we all learned body signing. So instead of Makaton which is visual, like for 'more' he would bang his shoulder, and 'finished' he would bang on the table. … And then things like his key person would have a certain perfume on her scarf that she wouldn't change, so that he could recognise her when he came in. We learned so much from him.*

Another leader explained how she had trialled video recording of a professional development tool. This captured moments of interaction between children and practitioners to inform an approach to individual education planning for children with particular SEND needs across two of her settings. She felt this to be beneficial to practitioner knowledge and understanding of the specific needs of each child. Another practitioner explained the way in which her setting had become especially knowledgeable about autism due to the interest and commitment of staff. This had led to the setting becoming an (unofficial) specialist provider for children with autism which enabled *'Children [to] come out of their own worlds and begin to seek social and emotional interaction with practitioners'*.

Many research participants cited offering training to other ECEC providers in their area, sharing SEND expertise. In fact, 98% head teachers and 70% of practitioners mentioned their involvement in providing training for other non-maintained settings and families in the local community more generally. The examples they drew on included:

- Providing advice and guidance, signposting parents to services and support.
- Running community accessible groups with focus on early language and home learning.
- Working alongside other agencies including health, social care, and education to support families to engage with services to protect and support vulnerable children.
- Delivering family-support sessions including managing challenging behaviour, early language skills, literacy, and maths sessions.

In addition, some interviewees mentioned delivering outreach programmes designed to meet with parents and children with complex SEND in the community through play sessions that involved both children and parents and carers.

Making an impact for SEND

Our data suggested that many MNS practitioners not only considered their role as concerned with the immediate impact they might have upon the child and the child's family but looked longer term for ways they might help a child transition from one context to another in later life. This head teacher explained the approach taken to developing SEND for life-long resilience so that:

> We deliberately work on a carousel [with all children in the nursery] so that when they [SEND children] do transition to a school, they're not dependent on one particular adult.

Our data presented many examples of ECPs recounting planning for a child's next steps, beyond the nursery to participate in wider community life. One leader described the time and effort that was put into developing individual education and health-care plans (IHCP) for children. Often these had to be drawn up knowing that the child would move on to mainstream school during the process, and that they would, nonetheless, have to find a way to carry the cost of the provision:

> And often we take them at massive expense to ourselves. Because, if a child is only here for a year, well, no one gets diagnosed in a year. And nobody gets an IHCP plan in a year. So we will support them [the children] one-to-one. ... I know all the nursery schools feel the same, you couldn't not take a child because it's not in the child's best interest to be knocking around at home, particularly one with significant special needs.

Much of the data foregrounded the everyday and wellbeing of the child in the context of their family and the impact for the wellbeing of the SEND in attending to the needs of wider family members. One head teacher told us about noticing that perhaps *'Mummy needs some support, too'* in terms of recognising parents' social and emotional needs.

Nonetheless, many head teachers felt that it was important to be able to account quantifiably for the leaps in achievement that children with SEND were able to make in their charge:

> ... there is a gap when they come ... then a vast majority of our children go out where they should be. And so it converts from being 13% on track on entry to being 70% on track on exit. And our SEND children make ... at least good progress, if not better. ... they make significant progress ... 90% are at age related expectation or above when they leave ... including children with disabilities, 90% of them are where they should be; excluding children with disabilities, 96% are where they should be or above.

The challenges to providing SEND good practice

The challenge of securing funding for children with SEND was a recurring theme of our data, and especially as this related to ongoing planning for the future needs of children and their families requiring knowledgeable and well-informed practitioners, as this MNS leader explained:

> *Maintained Nursery schools offer high quality education for the most vulnerable children in society. To do this, highly skilled professionals need to work together to keep updated with recent and relevant research striving for continuous improvement and growth. This requires investment in training and resourcing.*

Difficulties with securing funding for IHCPs were another recurring theme as was mention of not being able to access some grant funding streams available to the non-maintained sector. However, despite the frustrations, this leader expressed the determination of her practitioners to work for all children and those with SEND:

> *Much like many Early Childhood Practitioners across the ECEC sector, MNS staff work long hours, for pay that does not necessarily reflect the level of work ... [with a] commitment to improving children's outcomes, practitioners continue to provide quality care and education.*

Our data, similar to Paull and Popov (2019), demonstrated how MNSs were at risk of sustaining their support for all children and their families, and especially those with additional needs, vulnerabilities and SEND due to fiscal uncertainties and constraints. This question becomes more urgent in pandemic and post-pandemic contexts of fiscal public policy decision-making.

Conclusion

The MNS is ideally constituted and situated to attend to SEND with the knowledge and expertise of practitioners able to engage with children and their families; other maintained and non-maintained ECECs and the needs of children, placed as they often are within conurbations of need and social and economic deprivation in England. MNSs espouse a model of a community which necessarily values a network of practitioners, professionals, families, and wider members of communities to share concerns and passions, especially focused on the most vulnerable and those with the most challenging SEND. During the pandemic, for example, even after the government paused the shielding advice for children classed as Clinically, Extremely Vulnerable from 31 March 2021 (DfE 2021, p. 7), ECPs, regardless of their setting status, as maintained or non-maintained, continued to work with, and support SEND children and their families through digital learning platforms, demonstrating their versatility, commitment and skill in attending to the needs of SEND children.

> **REFLECTIVE POINTS**
>
> Consider your experience of working with children with SEND.
> Reflect upon any of the following as they apply to you:
>
> 1. Do you (and/or your setting) currently see working with a child with SEND as an opportunity for your own further development of skills and provision? Is this an area that you might develop?
> 2. What are the implications of reduced local authority funding on your setting's provision for children with SEND?
> 3. How do you currently work with parents and multi-agencies in identifying and supporting children with SEND? Are there areas you would like to improve or enhance? What are they and in what ways?

References

Alderson, P. (2018). How the rights of all school students and teachers are affected by special educational needs or disability (SEND) services: Teaching, psychology, policy. *London Review of Education*, 16 (2): 175–190. doi: 10.18546/LRE.16.2.01

Barton, L. (2005). Special educational needs – an alternative new look. https://disability-studies.leeds.ac.uk/wp-content/uploads/sites/40/library/Barton-Warnock.pdf

Borkett, P. (2021). *Special Educational Needs in the Early Years: A Guide to Inclusive Practice*. London: Sage Publications Ltd.

Department for Education. (2014). *Early years: guide to the 0 to 25 SEND code of practice: Advice for early years providers that are funded by the local authority*. https://assets.publishing.service.gov.uk/government/uploads/system/uploads/attachment_data/file/350685/Early_Years_Guide_to_SEND_Code_of_Practice_-_02Sept14.pdf

Department for Education and Department of Health. (DfE and DoH). (2015). *Special educational needs and disability code of practice: 0 to 25 years Statutory guidance for organisations which work with and support children and young people who have special educational needs or disabilities.* https://assets.publishing.service.gov.uk/government/uploads/system/uploads/attachment_data/file/398815/SEND_Code_of_Practice_January_2015.pdf

Department for Education. (2017a). *Statutory Framework for the Early Years Foundation Stage.* https://www.gov.uk/government/publications/early-years-foundation-stage-framework--2

Department for Education. (2017b*). Early Years Workforce Strategy*. https://assets.publishing.service.gov.uk/government/uploads/system/uploads/attachment_data/file/596884/Workforce_strategy_02-03-2017.pdf

Department for Education. (2021). *SEND and Specialist Settings – Additional Operational Guidance: COVID-19.* https://assets.publishing.service.gov.uk/government/uploads/system/uploads/attachment_data/file/984861/FINAL_cleared_SEND_Guidance_10_May.pdf

Early Education. (2015). *Maintained Nursery Schools: The State of Play Report.* https://www.early-education.org.uk/sites/default/files/Nursery%20Schools%20State%20of%20Play%20Report%20final%20print.pdf

Early Education. (2018). *First Choice and Last Resort: The Unique Role of Maintained Nursery Schools in England in Supporting Children with Special Educational Needs and Disabilities (SEND).* https://www.early-education.org.uk/sites/default/files/SEND%20in%20MNS%20survey%20findings%20Sept%202018.pdf

Frederick, K. (2005). 'Let's take the special out of special needs', *Times Educational Supplement*, 15 July, 19.

Hodkinson, A. (2010). Inclusive and special education in the English educational system: Historical perspectives, recent developments and future challenges. *British Journal of Special Education*, 37 (2): 61–67. https://doi.org/10.1111/j.1467-8578.2010.00462.x

Oliver, M. (1990). *The Politics of Disablement.* Basingstoke: Macmillan

Pascal, C. and Bertram, T. (2019). *The Unique and Added Value of Birmingham's Maintained Nurser Schools.* http://www.crec.co.uk/announcements/unique-hidden-value-birmingham-mns

Paull, G. and Popov, D. (2019). *The Role and Contribution of Maintained Nursery Schools in the Early Years Sector in England.* https://assets.publishing.service.gov.uk/government/uploads/system/uploads/attachment_data/file/912995/Frontier_Economics_MNS_report_REVISED_v2.pdf

Solvason, C. and Proctor, S. (2021) 'You have to find the right words to be honest': nurturing relationships between teachers and parents of children with Special Educational Needs. *Support for Learning*, 36(3): 470–485.

Solvason, C., Webb, R., and Sutton-Tsang, S. (2020). *Evidencing the Effects of Maintained Nursery Schools' Roles in Early Years Sector Improvements.* https://imx07wlgmj301rre1jepv8h0-wpengine.netdna-ssl.com/wp-content/uploads/2020/03/MNS-Research-Report.pdf

Warnock, M. (1978). *Special Educational Needs: Report of the Committee of Enquiry into the Education of Handicapped Children and Young People.* London: HMSO.

UNESCO. (1994). *The Salamanca Statement and Framework for Action on Special Needs Education.* Paris: UNESCO.

6
RE-IMAGINING EARLY CHILDHOOD PEDAGOGY

Johanna Cliffe

Introduction

Urban (2008, p. 136) starts his discussion of Early Childhood Practitioner (ECP) identity with this quote from Winnicott (1987, p. 15 cited in Urban, 2008, p. 135): 'To begin with, you will be relieved to know that I am not going to tell you what to do'. Although this may seem a peculiar choice, it is important to remember, as Solvason, Webb and Sutton-Tsang (2020) identify, that ECPs are dedicated, knowledgeable and skillful professionals. Strong pedagogic knowledge is the cornerstone of EC practice; ECPs are educators, guides and advocates for children through their crucial, early years. Simply put, ECPs are experts within their field, despite often being silenced or subverted within hegemonic discourse. Moss (2019) suggests that the challenge within early childhood education and care (ECEC) is not with the workforce itself (many of you reading this) but rather the difficulty of functioning within a system that tends towards discrediting existing ECP professional knowledge and expertise, whilst simultaneously seeking to reinvent it within a narrow preprescribed and sanctioned image under the guise of professionalisation.

Who gets to decide 'what counts as professional knowledge' at any one particular time is a polemic issue, linked to sociocultural and political official discourse (Barron, 2016, p. 326). Therefore, this chapter seeks to (re)position the ECP as a multifaceted, complex and knowledgeable educator: someone who can be recognised through 'official' discourses championed at any one moment in time, whilst also being much more besides. The chapter demonstrates how ECP subjectivities enact a range of alternative pedagogic approaches that can be, and often are, employed within ECEC, to resist and challenge some reductive and dominant discourses.

When any ECP identity, or pedagogic approach, becomes a dominant discourse, it risks becoming a Foucauldian regime of truth (1980 cited in Cohen 2008, p. 9),

DOI: 10.4324/9781003206262-7

functioning as the *only way* rather than one of many ways to engage with young children in ECEC. This *only way*, as set out in *Early Years Foundation Stage* (EYFS) (Department for Education, DfE, 2021) with specific and known 'end points', is somewhat paradoxical; the same document also champions a diversity within both pace and approach, promoting a unique individualism inherent in the ECEC and the sociocultural theorisations that this presumes. The conflict between uniqueness and the normative and developmental assumptions of the statutory EY documentation (DfE, 2017, DfE, 2021) is clear. Deleuze and Guattari's (1987) philosophy suggests there are multiple pathways to many 'truths', of being a 'successful' young child in an ECEC setting. We owe it to the diverse children and families we work with to accommodate ways of seeing, experiencing, and interacting with their worlds that validate what they think, see and do in order to provide a more equitable and socially just educational start in life for them.

Applying Deleuzio-Guattarian (1987) metaphorical concepts such as the rhizome and nomad provides a coherent way forward in (re)conceiving multiplicities within pedagogy and practice and ways of *being* in ECEC as an ECP. Rhizomes have multiple connections that travel in any and all directions: they never retrace their pathways; instead they are constantly (re)evolving via multiple entries and exits to regenerate and (de/re)territorialise new routes. This is an idea taken up by Hayes and Filipović (2018, p. 225), who note that 'it is the process of travelling the pathways rather than the destination' that is important, acknowledging that within ECEC the co-collaborations of knowledge and relational experiences play a more crucial role than the normative endpoint. When combined with the concept of nomad which embodies movement, adaptability and freedom, the focus is taken away from beginnings and endings of learning; the journey itself becomes paramount and the focus for the ECP shifts to the interactions within and between the interconnected make-up of pedagogic encounters.

Adopting a nomadic stance empowers ECPs to resist fixed and binary positions of one identity to enter a world of possibility, a 'domain of potentialities full of unpredictable becomings' (Moss, 2019, p. 118). The nomad is free to follow the rhizomatic nature and voice of 'Other', whatever form Other might take; child, colleague, parent or carer are just some examples. This opens up learning as an opportunity for both ECP and Other to find out and evolve *together* in partnership; to discover the new and insightful rather than merely engaging in (re)representations of what has gone before, and the 'tried and tested'.

These Deleuzio-Guattarian (1987) concepts offer opportunities for ECPs to justify flexible conceptual spaces in their interactions; to feel confident when they stop and pay attention to the multiplicity and complexity of the moment, uncovering the potential of many layers of meaning and connections constructed relationally by children and ECPs in the materiality of their environment. This (re)imagining and (re)conceptualising practice allows space to ask critically challenging questions, such as what else exists here? How does it work? 'and... and... and' (Deleuze and Guattari, 1987). This approach resists and challenges face value, taken-for-granted, one-size-fits-all dominant EYFS discourses and assumptions of 'how to be' a recognisably competent ECP. It opens up to potentials and possibilities, to the remarkable and the different; , essentially enabling space for the unique.

Context … what we have now …

Urban (2008, p. 136) proposes that ECPs have the skills and capacities to 'act concretely, spontaneously and autonomously in ever-changing, uncertain situations … often beyond practitioner control'. Hayes and Filipović (2018, p. 221) similarly recognise the ability of ECPs to acknowledge and accommodate the uniqueness of every child and every moment with every child; stating 'young children learn in holistic, embodied and integrated ways as they develop and make sense of their world'. Fundamentally, the role of the ECP is a complex and constant navigation of competing pedagogic imperatives. Yet, despite this innate professionalism and adaptability, the complexity of the role of the ECP is rarely recognised and respected; nor is their 'specialised knowledge' (Brock, 2013, p. 36) regarding the 'sophisticated nuances' (Hayes and Filipović, 2018, p. 228) of children's early learning and development.

Brock (2013, p. 37) suggests that EC 'practitioners' dialogue has not always been valued highly', as it is often 'judged as being a tacit understanding rather than professional knowledge'. Likewise, Brock (2013), Barron (2016) and Basford (2019) argue that ECPs struggle to be seen and heard, to articulate their situated knowledge, in the face of top-down opposition and the 'cacophony of competing discourse' (Barron, 2016, p. 335). Consequently, the voices of ECPs are often silenced or subverted, culminating in a loss of their own subjective agency and autonomy within pedagogical discourse.

Ironically, the uniqueness of ECEC became threatened when its value was recognised. Longitudinal research projects, such as the *Effective Provision of Preschool Education* (EPPE) (Sylva et al., 2004) and *Researching Effective Pedagogy in the Early Years* (REPEY) (Siraj-Blatchford et al., 2002), clearly evidenced the correlation between strong pedagogic practice and effective outcomes for young children. Later, follow-up research by Sylva et al. (2014) drew parallels with high-quality early provision in relation to longer-term attainment, at GCSEs and beyond. This bolstered the importance of ECEC and, according to Gibson (2015), placed unprecedented importance on *where* and with *whom* children spend their first crucial years. Quality ECEC provision became synonymous with children's attainment; therefore, EC pedagogy became entwined with performance discourse (Gibson, 2015).

Hayes and Filipović (2018), Moss (2019) and Moss and Cameron (2020) all argue that the rationale for increased government gaze and investment is a socio-economic one. They reason that ECEC is being consumed within a top-down, neoliberal ideology, one that prioritises universality, rationalism and essentialism, in an attempt to ensure greater economic returns. Discourses relating to attachment, the impacts of early experiences and addressing socio-economic disadvantage and child poverty, have become entwined with a measurement and outcomes-driven agenda with a focus upon enabling 'the most disadvantaged to escape social deprivation' (Barron, 2016, p. 327).

From 2011, EY settings were included in Ofsted inspections, leading to what Roberts-Holmes (2015, p. 306) refers to as a 'data-driven pedagogy'; a far cry from the unique child and child-centred principles espoused within and by the sector. As a consequence, a practice dissonance has emerged; as ECPs are in the dichotomous and paradoxical position of attempting to balance care and education, whilst reconciling both within 'future-focused outcome driven' discourses (Hayes and Filipović, 2018, p. 221; Basford, 2019). Inevitably it is care, which has no form of extrinsic measure, that is most likely to be sacrificed in the ideological prioritisation of value.

Henshall et al. (2018) suggest a key issue for ECPs is a general misunderstanding of the pedagogical underpinnings of EY practice by policy makers and within the wider educative field. This diminishes ECP expertise and actively prevents ECPs from 'enacting their professionalism' (ibid, p. 423). Corroboratively, Moss and Cameron (2020) argue the emergence of developmentally appropriate practice (DAP) and the school readiness' or 'schoolification' agenda within the UK and other Western-informed societies, has eclipsed other EY pedagogical approaches: despite these paradigms being the antithesis of effective EY pedagogy. *Starting Strong: Early Education and Care* (Organisation for Economic Cooperation and Development, OECD, 2001) argued that schoolification adopts a reductive view of early education, whilst potentially prioritising inappropriate EY pedagogical practice. The report further states that 'the divisions between care and education are meaningless', as the purpose of ECEC is not to influence school performance, but to focus on quality experiences in the 'here and now' (ibid., p. 42).

The problem is that more complex knowledge of social critiques of normative development, such as play-based ways of discovering and evolving, do not 'fit' straightforwardly with the neoliberal ideals that underpin the technical rationale required of educational settings in the UK. With increasing attempts to regulate and standardise ECEC, there is a danger that pedagogical ECP expertise and established, invaluable EY practice will be buried under the weight of top-down developmental and cognitive discourses. This imposed reality risks not only the loss of diverse ECP knowledge and expertise but also the very real potential of losing sight of the complex and relational child, in the competing arena of social capital and economic globalisation (Hayes and Filipović, 2018; Basford, 2019; Moss, 2019; Moss and Cameron, 2020).

Through a Deleuze (1994, p. 27) lens, the pedagogic voice of the ECP has become 'Other' and at practice and policy level it is gradually being seized and misappropriated to function as the 'Same'. This channelling into the Same risks eroding pedagogic knowledge and ECP professionalism into a compliant ECP, whilst simultaneously composing a pedagogic blueprint of the normal' child (Langford, 2010; Lenz Taguchi, 2010; Cliffe and Solvason, 2016, 2019). Again, this leaves the ECP in a pedagogically paradoxical position where professionalism, values-led practice and the unique needs of the child, family, and community conflict with regulatory and statutory requirements.

Considering alternative pedagogies ...

Lenz-Taguchi (2010) asks how, in an age where our understanding about children's complex and multifaceted sociocultural ways of being has grown considerably, we have ended up with a normative, one-size-fits-all, approach within ECEC. The answer would seem to lie in Western society's subscription to the ideology of a knowledge-acquisition-based economy where knowledge, social capital and power have become intertwined. From this perspective children's learning occupies an epistemological position inspired by cognition and cognitive theory, developmentally appropriate practice (DAP) and developmental psychology. The pedagogic underpinning of these approaches, at first glance, support child-centred principles and, therefore, can be mistakenly viewed as promoting diverse and inclusive practice (Lenz-Taguchi, 2010). Yet, in actuality they are geared toward a narrowing of targets to fulfil a normative agenda.

Even if we bear in mind the debate around the appropriateness of child-centred practices, child-centred and DAP approaches merely serve to codify and classify learning into binary right/wrong ways to learn and predictable predetermined pathways to sense and meaning. Essentially, they are enacted through future-focused outcomes driven curricula focused on reproduction rather than innovation and creativity (Moss, 2019 p. 110). Consequently, innovation, creative thought, diversity and difference within learning become marginalised; children merely retread pre-known learning pathways to meet predetermined assessment outcomes in a linear fashion. There are no spaces for the child's or the ECP's own rhizomatic tracks. Deleuze (1994) suggests this pedagogic approach to education simply promotes binary dichotomies and fixed and entrenched positions, producing linear layers to learning and development. Cagliari et al. (2016, p. 421) refer to this rather aptly as 'prophetic pedagogy'; an approach that claims an omnipotent all-knowing foundation: a rather incongruous pedagogical stance when dealing with the complex phenomenon of young children's emergence and the unpredictable reality of daily practices. They go on to claim such approaches are both 'humiliating to teachers' ingenuity and a complete and visible humiliation of children's ingenuity and potential' (ibid., p. 422). Cameron (2020, p. 110) echoes the call of many frontline ECPs, for a broader and more encompassing view of EY pedagogy; one that encompasses the holistic nature of early childhood evolution and socialisation and one that further reconciles and reinstates the interrelational concepts of care and education.

The interwoven care and education nexus is championed by Cameron (2020, p. 101) who suggests a new ECP role, that of social pedagogue. Similarly, Basford (2019) discusses the benefits of relational pedagogy, a concept which is encapsulated within Hayes and Filipović's (2018, p. 222) notion of a nurturing pedagogy. The common factor assumed within these alternative pedagogic paradigms is the (re)positioning of focus away from cognition and DAP to pedagogic encounters where sense and meaning are cooperatively created and emerge within relational interactions. In some cases, as is well known in Reggio Emilia influenced provision, this also reimagines the purpose of assessment documentation. Cowan and Flewitt

(2020, p. 178) discuss how children, parents or carers and ECPs within Reggio settings work collaboratively to produce pedagogic documentation that is not merely evidence for standardised assessments, but an ongoing negotiated and constantly (re)evolving reflection of young children's interests, knowledge, thoughts and meaning making. Within pedagogic documentation, insights are skilfully interpreted by ECPs with children playing an active role. Learning becomes a democratic process with a valuing of the idea of equal partnership. Assessment becomes a negotiated process undertaken *with* children, rather than one that is *done to* or *done on* children.

So what does this mean in practice?

It could be argued that none of these concepts are new to the field of ECEC. In fact, Cameron (2020) explains that, whilst UK policy considered and rejected this approach when it was identified within the Children's Workforce Strategy (DfES, 2005), the social pedagogue already functions effectively in Denmark and New Zealand and within Reggio-Emilia informed practices. Embedding principles of individuality and creativity within the curriculum has not proved a problem elsewhere in the world. Dalli (2011), for example, discusses the benefits of the Te Whariki (Ministry of Education, 2017) curriculum in New Zealand, which acknowledges the social, cultural and historic values inherent in the differing New Zealand communities, whilst respecting ECP's specialist knowledge in allowing them control over content and delivery. Hargraves (2014) explored the theories which underpin the Te Whariki curriculum and discovered that whilst they are primarily constructivist in nature, they also consider social and sociocultural pedagogic influences and national cultural identity. This is in stark contrast to the schoolification approach and neoliberal idealism favoured by the UK and other Western-informed societies.

Within alternative pedagogic readings, a closer exploration of play and child-centred approaches reveals interwoven threads of relational and nurturing pedagogy, and even a version of the social pedagogue. For example, the tenets of play-based pedagogy, alongside the unique child and child-centred paradigms are tenaciously upheld by ECPs within ECEC despite this often being seen as *just* play outside of the sector (McMillian, 2017; Sproule, Walsh and McGuinness, 2019). The EYFS (DfE, 2021, p. 16) states

> play is essential for children's development, building their confidence as they learn to explore, relate to others, set their own goals and solve problems. Children learn by leading their own play, and by taking part in play which is guided by adults.

However, Sproule, Walsh and McGuinness (2019, p. 409) suggest that tension remains between 'play pedagogy' and 'direct teaching' with playfulness' becoming an uneasy compromise between the two. They go on to discuss the 'playful professional'; an ECP who is comfortable sharing the power within a relational encounter to become a flexible and curious co-explorer (ibid., p. 420). McMillian (2017, p. 205) describes the playful professional as a demanding role; one that is 'not a task for amateurs' due to the sophisticated balancing act of professionalism, 'with so many roles and interactions needing to be managed simultaneously' (ibid.). This multifaceted and complex view of play pedagogy and the playful pedagogue is rather ironic when, as previously stated, it is an aspect of the ECP role that is often misunderstood and derided as 'less than' in educational policy contexts.

The playful ECP persona, in many ways, embodies the concept of Deleuze and Guattari's (1987) nomad, acknowledging and accommodating the intricacies of the playful assemblage and accepting the possibility of a rhizomatic journey. A playful pedagogue recognises that pedagogic and playful encounters are relational and while they need to be reconciled within regulatory assessment frameworks, they cannot be eclipsed by policy dictates. However, embracing a playful persona is not always natural or easy as it requires a willingness to embrace the potentially unknown and unpredictable, which can be a disconcerting process for some. Page (2017, p. 391) suggests that ECPs need to 'possess the intellectual capacity and emotional resilience' to fully embrace and embody relational encounters with children.

There is always the temptation to grasp the 'Otherness' within playful encounters and by doing so, risk (re)framing it into something known, familiar, comfortable and recognisable, basically mutating 'Other' into the 'Same' (Moss, 2019, pp. 110–111). Through a feminist 'ethic of care' lens (Tronto, 2013; Noddings, 2015) and the postmodern lens of 'ethics of an encounter' (Levinus, 1987, cited in Moss, 2019, pp. 60–62), the responsibility for Other emerges. ECPs assume the role of advocate and protector of Other, resisting turning it into Same, or eclipsing Other within prophetic pedagogy. Feminist and postmodern paradigms serve to resist 'hyper-dominant' EY discourses and also fundamentally identify what it might *mean* to be responsible for young children. This is especially important when 'measurable outcomes discourses influence parental and societal understandings and expectations of ECEC' (Hayes and Filipović, 2018, p. 224), pulling the focus away from specialist EY pedagogic discourses towards a normative schoolification agenda (Moss and Cameron, 2020). Enacting an ethic of care would ensure the relational pedagogic nature inherent in encounters with young children was respected and interrelational. This supposition should be a cornerstone of ECEC pedagogic practice enacted by the knowledgeable ECP; however, it is not easily reconciled within the one-size-fits-all approach.

A pedagogic perspective that acknowledges the complex and diverse ECP within ECEC practice will influence whether a resolution in reconciling care and education can be enacted. Hayes and Filipović (2018, p. 222) argue that a nurturing pedagogy accommodates this, as it attempts to embody care, education, playful interaction and dialogue, alongside authentic co-collaborative learning and pedagogic encounters. It could be further argued to have aspects of relational ethics (Basford, 2019) and the social pedagogue (Cameron, 2020).

It appears logical from Hayes and Filipović (2018) discussions to assume that a nurturing pedagogy may be one way to bridge the pedagogic gap between care and education and provide an alternative to the 'future-focused outcome driven' discourse that is pressing in on ECEC currently. This may in turn offer a more equitable and socially just approach to ECEC for the ECP, the child, their family and community.

Conclusion ... what next?

By considering the Deleuzo-Guattarian (1987) notion of the rhizome and applying the concept of nomad, the fixed and binary positions of one pathway to truth, sense and meaning can be avoided and the multifaceted role of the ECP championed. Although this chapter has presented DAP and an over-focus on cognitive theory and knowledge reproduction in a more negative light, the issue is not with the approaches themselves but with the once-size-fits-all paradigm they promote. As Dewey (1910, p. 12) once asserted: it is not about finding ways to 'think harder ... but to think differently'. What is needed is not an 'anti' approach which feeds binary right/wrong fixed positions, but a pedagogic bridge that supports as many remarkable, different and unique pathways to learning and 'being a child' as possible. Children have a hundred languages and as the poem highlights, we rob them of ninety-nine (Cagliari et al., 2016) when we should be acknowledging and accommodating as many as is possible.

ECPs must navigate a complex reality within ECEC working, within a discourse that neither understands nor fully appreciates their variety of 'specialised knowledge' (Brock, 2013, p. 36), and the 'sophisticated nuances' (Hayes and Filipović, 2018, p. 228) prevalent within young children's learning in their crucial first years. Having a coherent way forward to accommodate pedagogic multiplicity and the freedom to enact their professionalism is essential if ECEC is to continue to provide for and safeguard the wellbeing of our youngest children.

REFLECTIVE POINTS

This chapter not only called for a (re)imagining of EY pedagogy but also a (re)positioning of the ECP within ECEC education. This (re)positioning often starts with our own understandings of who we are as ECPs.

Consider your own professional identity as an ECP and reflect on the following:

- What pedagogic approaches do you feel underpin your practice?
- Where have these come from and why do you believe them to be of importance for your own professional development and for the learning and development of the children in your care?
- How do your professional ideals and professional identity relate to your pedagogic practice? Are there any tensions?
- After reading this chapter, are there any aspects of your practice where you feel you might like to 'think differently'? What are these and why?

References

Barron, I. (2016) 'Flight turbulence: the stormy professional trajectory of trainee early years' teachers in England', *International Journal of Early Years Education*, 24(3), pp. 325–341.

Basford, J. (2019) 'Being a graduate professional in the field of Early Childhood Education and Care: silence, submission and subversion', *Education 3-13*, 47(7), pp. 862–875.

Brock, A. (2013) 'Building a model of early years professionalism from practitioners' perspectives', *Journal of Early Childhood Research*, 11 (1), pp. 27–44.

Cagliari, P., Castagnetti, M., Giudici, C., and Rinaldi, C. (2016) *Loris Malaguzzi and the schools of Reggio Emilia: A selection of his writings and speeches, 1945-1993*. London: Routledge.

Cameron, C. (2020) 'Towards a rich ECEC workforce', in Moss, P. and Cameron, C. (eds.) *Transforming early childhood in England: towards a democratic education*. London: University College Press, pp. 101–122.

Cliffe, J., and Solvason, C. (2016) *Using rhizomatic thinking in early childhood pedagogy to avoid making other into the same*. Retrieved from http://tactyc.org.uk/reflections

Cliffe, J., and Solvason, C. (2019) 'Should we consider rhizomatic thinking when educating young minds?' *NZ International Research in Early Childhood Education Journal*, 22(1), pp. 86–100.

Cohen, L.E. (2008) 'Foucault and the early childhood classroom', *Educational Studies: A Journal of the American Educational Studies Association*, 44(1), pp. 7–21

Cowan, K., and Flewitt, R. (2020) 'Towards valuing children's signs of learning', in Moss, P. and Cameron, C. (eds.) *Transforming early childhood in England: towards a democratic education*. London: University College Press, pp. 169–187.

Dalli, C. (2011) 'A curriculum of open possibilities: a New Zealand kindergarten teacher's view of professional practice.' *Early Years Journal of International Research*, 31 (3), pp. 229–243.

Deleuze, G. (1994 reprinted 2014) *Difference and repetition* (2nd edn). London: Bloomsbury.

Deleuze, G., and Guattari, F. (1987, reprinted 2013) *A thousand plateaus*. London: Bloomsbury.

Department for Education (DfE) (2021) *Statutory framework for the early years foundation stage: setting the standards for learning, development and care for children from birth to five*. Department of Education Publication, Available at: https://assets.publishing.service.gov.uk/government/uploads/system/uploads/attachment_data/file/974907/EYFS_framework_-_March_2021.pdf (Accessed: 4 February 2022).

Department for Education and Skills (DfES) (2005) *Children's workforce strategy*. Nottingham: Department for Education and Skills.

Dewey, J. (1910 reprinted 2015) *How we think* (Kindle addition). Some good Press.

Gibson, M. (2015) 'Heroic victims: discursive constructions of preservice early childhood teacher professional identities', *Journal of Early Childhood Teacher Education*, 36(2), pp. 142–155.

Hargraves, V. 2014. 'Complex possibilities: working theories as an outcome for the early childhood curriculum', *Contemporary issues in Early Childhood*, 15(4), pp. 319–328.

Hayes, N., and Filipović, K. (2018) 'Nurturing "buds of development": from outcomes to opportunities in early childhood practice', *International Journal of Early Years Education*, 26 (3), pp. 220–232.

Henshall, A., Atkins, L., Bolan, R., Harrison, J., and Munn, H. (2018) 'Certified to make a difference: The motivations and perceptions of newly qualified early years teachers in England', *Journal of Vocational Education and Training*, 70(3), pp. 417–434.

Langford, R. (2010), 'Critiquing child-centred pedagogy to bring children and early childhood educators into the centre of a democratic pedagogy', *Contemporary Issues in Early Childhood*, 11(1), pp. 113–127.

Lenz-Taguchi, H. (2010) 'Rethinking pedagogical practices in early childhood education: a multidimensional approach to learning and inclusion', in Yelland, N. (eds) *Contemporary perspectives in early childhood education*. Berkshire: McGraw-Hill, pp. 14–33.

McMillian, D. (2017) 'Towards the playful professional', in Walsh, G., McMillian, D., and McGuinness, C. (eds.) *Playful teaching and learning*. London: Sage, pp. 198–213.

Ministry of Education (2017) Te Whāriki He whāriki mātauranga mō ngā mokopuna o Aotearoa: Early childhood curriculum. Available at: https://www.education.govt.nz/assets/Documents/Early-Childhood/ELS-Te-Whariki-Early-Childhood-Curriculum-ENG-Web.pdf (Accessed 19 July 2022).

Moss, P. (2019) *Alternative narratives in early childhood: an introduction for students and practitioners*. Oxon: Routledge.

Moss, P., and Cameron, C. (2020) *Transforming early childhood in England: towards a democratic education*. London: University College Press.

Noddings N. (2015) 'Care ethics and caring organisations', in Engster, D., and Hamington, M. (eds.) *Care ethics and political theory*. Oxford: University Press, pp. 72–84.

Organisation for Economic Cooperation and Development (OECD). (2001) *Starting strong early childhood education and care*. OEDC publication Available at: https://read.oecd-ilibrary.org/education/starting-strong_9789264192829-en#page213 (Accessed 5 October 2020).

Page, J. (2017) 'Reframing infant-toddler pedagogy through a lens of professional love: exploring narratives of professional practice in early childhood settings in England', *Contemporary Issues in Early Childhood*, 18(4), pp. 387–399.

Roberts-Holmes, G. (2015) 'The 'datafication' of early years pedagogy: 'if the teaching is good, the data should be good and if there's bad teaching, there is bad data'', *Journal of Education Policy*, 30(3), pp. 302–315.

Siraj-Blatchford, I., Sylva, K., Muttock, S., Gilden, R., and Bell, D. (2002) *Researching effective pedagogy in the early years*. Available at: http://dera.ioe.ac.uk/4650/1/RR356.pdf (Accessed: 5 October 2020).

Solvason, C., Webb, R., and Sutton-Tsang, S. (2020) *Evidencing the effects of maintained nursery schools' roles in Early Years sector improvements*. Available at https://tactyc.org.uk/research/ (Accessed: 7th February 2022)

Sproule, L., Walsh, G., and McGuinness, C. (2019) 'More than "just play": Picking out three dimensions of a balanced early years pedagogy', *International Journal of Early Years Education*, 27(4), pp. 409–422.

Sylva, K., Melhuish, E., Sammons, P., Siraj-Blatchford, I., Taggart, B., and Elliot, K. (2004) *The effective provision of pre-school education project*. London: DfES.

Sylva, K., Melhuish, E., Sammons, P., Siraj-Blatchford, I., Taggart, B., Elliot, K., Smees, R., Toth, K., Welcomme, W., and Hollingworth, K. (2014) *Students' educational and developmental outcomes at age 16: Effective Pre-school, Primary and Secondary Education (EPPSE 3-16) Project*. Department for Education Publication, Available at: https://assets.publishing.service.gov.uk/government/uploads/system/uploads/attachment_data/file/351499/RB354_-_Students__educational_and_developmental_outcomes_at_age_16_Brief.pdf (Accessed: 5 October 2020).

Tronto, J.C. (2013) *Caring democracy markets equality, and justice*. London: University Press.

Urban, M. (2008) 'Dealing with uncertainty: challenges and possibilities for the early childhood profession', *European Early Childhood Education Research Journal*, 16(2), pp. 135–152.

7
NURTURING NATURE WITH(IN) CHILDREN (OR 'GEORGE KILLED THE WORM')

Kathleen Bailey

Introduction

This chapter explores and celebrates the dynamic skill, sensibilities and responsibilities required of Early Childhood Practitioners (ECPs) when they recognise themselves as a child nature-nurturer within Early Childhood Education and Care (ECEC) settings. To do this I present a 'story' that reflects one way in which children engage with nature in an outdoor (educational) setting. The story, from my own research with young children, indicates the complexity and subtlety required of ECPs when negotiating children's experience of nature in a way that marries this to a wider political context of environmental sustainability. Therefore, it exemplifies a way that ECPs might champion a conceptual framing for the child, with a focus upon the ethic of inter-species justice, without reverting to 'telling' children what to think and how to behave. This way of practising embraces the ethic of exploration underpinning much ECEC practice and celebrates pedagogy beyond the constraints of a technicist approach.

Implicit to my approach to ECEC pedagogy and research is Taylor and Giugni's (2012, p. 102) suggestion of taking up a 'common worlds pedagogy' where 'inclusion' assumes more than human perspectives as productive in the creation of knowledge with young children. This is a way ECPs might add to their own thinking and reflective practices as they spend time with children, considering the world through the lenses of other species, trees, rocks and other material and non-material bodies and forces. This approach assumes that the more-than-human world might be included in what creates lived reality on planet Earth, as part of a multi-species caring environment. Taylor and Giugni (2012) argue that this post-humanist perspective (that looks beyond the human) might enable children to live compassionately and responsibly in a world viewed, at least scientifically, to be lacking capacity (in

DOI: 10.4324/9781003206262-8

terms of land, water and resources) to support ongoing human population growth, and thus ensure the future survival of humanity.

Nature in ECEC (at present)

Ideas of 'nature' and 'sustainability' are creeping to the foreground in ECEC practice, linked to a normative view that 'nature is good' for children (Bailey, 2019). This has the capacity to shape settings through predominant market mechanisms of parental demand (Lyndon, 2019). I perceive two distinct dimensions to the 'nature is good' view; the first, discernible in media stories (Coles, 2016; Hinds, 2019; Magee, 2017) and a wide range of research literature (Bento and Dias, 2017; Chawla, 2015; Maller, 2009), that nature is beneficial for children's holistic development and learning; physical and mental health; and well-being, including ideas of building resilience and self-esteem. The second seems antidotal (i.e. acting as an antidote) that nature works to alleviate a seemingly growing anxiety towards sustainability and other social issues as Louv's (2016) publication, *The Essential Guide to a Nature-Rich Life: 500 Ways to Enrich Your Family's Health & Happiness*, seems to suggest.

This construction of nature as 'good' positions children as crucial for creating a more sustainable world both now and in the future (Weldemariam et al., 2017). This is visible in the argument that children's exposure to nature leads automatically to their desire and ability to protect the natural environment (Chawla, 2015; Louv, 2010). In this vein, Louv (2010) campaigns for reinserting children, who he describes as deficit in nature, back into nature. Taylor (2013) questions the efficacy of this strategy as being grounded in white Western male perspectives of past childhoods. Weldermariam et al. (2017) note that despite this social discourse and wider framing of nature as good, there is no guidance for practice related to sustainability within the Statutory *Framework for the Early Years Foundation Stage* (EYFS; DFE, 2021); however, the notion that sustainability has relevance for ECEC is acknowledged in *Birth to Five Matters* (2021) guidance, compiled by the ECEC sector itself. Perhaps this suggests that the statutory EYFS and its non-statutory guidance, the new Development Matters (DfE, 2021), have yet to engage with emerging discourses, where nature is viewed as something that is necessary for children to engage with in connection with their emerging sustainable thinking. McLeod and Giardiello (2019), and Biesta (2016) discuss Aristotle's concept that educators have a role in creating what is educationally desirable. This should respond to the world views of their immediate communities, including parents and carers, but may be at odds with statutory policies which focus on normative outputs. Regardless of such barriers, a construction of 'nature as good' offers ECPs opportunities to draw on their knowledge and expertise to engage with nature for the benefit of both children and nature.

Methodology

This research is shaped by a social constructionist view that children create their own ideas about nature. Environmental historian Ramachandra Guha (2006) makes a case for the way humans construct nature as instrumental to environmentalist understandings that inform their views of 'sustainability'. Such a view chimes with Christians's (2018) notion that ethics, or moral codes, evolve from within communities. The research aimed, therefore, to witness an 'ethic of sustainability' as it emerged from child participants engaging with nature whilst simultaneously affected by the dynamics of the different and multiple communities, to which they belonged. This provides a useful framework for rethinking some of childhood studies' fundamental tenets and assumptions.

Data is presented through vignettes (Taylor and Pacini-Ketchabaw, 2015) drawing on the storying concepts of van Dooren (2016) and Blaise et al. (2017). Van Dooren (2016) uses 'the lively story' to draw attention to endangered species by bringing them 'alive', giving them 'vitality, presence perhaps "thickness" on the page and in the minds and lives of the readers' (van Dooren, 2016, p. 8). Inspired by the Reggio Emilia's concepts of pedagogic documentation and listening to children (Davies, 2014b), art-making was used for its ability to facilitate communication with young children. My notion of art-making is conceptually broad, and includes play as performance art, based on the idea that pretending and acting out roles are fundamental to children's play (Haughton and Ellis, 2016) enabling insights 'into the social worlds of children' (James and James, 2011, p. 11).

Sessions took place in a Forest School area in a local park, set up by myself, where I conduct after-school Forest School sessions. My workplace as an ECP lies within the vicinity of the park community; hence, I have known some of the child participants since they were toddlers; others I know only in my capacity as a Forest School practitioner or volunteer in the park. In addition, my nine-year-old son was sometimes present, joining in art-making alongside other participants. My relationships to the participants are significant, in that they produced different types of pedagogic relationships that affected analysis and are represented in the story of children's encounters with nature that follows. This is deliberately constructed to take readers into the messy, entangled material and embodied world of the child which includes play partners such as other children, other species, and myself as pedagogue, researcher and carer. The story embraces snippets of dialogue, explanation and analysis that generate a picture of one way in which children (and adults) might live responsibly with other species.

George and the worms: A story about inter-species justice:

GEORGE: *'That's Milo worm'* [audible in background]

This was the first mention of worms; it preceded a sequence of loosely bounded intra-actions of varying durations evolving around George, which together create the basis for this story about other species. As I pondered George's intra-actions with worms, it occurred to me that there was more going on than a child's fascination with bugs. It seemed that these intra-actions, between myself, the children, the worms and George, played out roles within a community that seem to fit notions of judge and jury, the police, the 'victim' (worm) and the individual (George) whom we all seek to bring into line with an unarticulated moral code or law.

Analysis in this case involved creating a storyboard where every intra-action relating to George and the worms was assembled on an A2 board. This enabled me to see all the intra-actions at once so that I might make connections, spot similarities and ponder ways in which a phenomenon becomes clear (which I refer to as 'interspecies justice'). The children involved here attended previous Forest School sessions in the park, and I have known Isabella, Daisy and Violet since they were toddlers. My son Milo was also present. The story is told chronologically with subheadings to indicate where positionings of judge and jury, victim, police, and individual emerge as the story unfolds.

Judge and Jury:

GEORGE: *Wormy, wormy, wormy, wormy, wormy!*
DAISY: *Kathleen, George found a wormy*
ME: *I hope he's going to take care of it, let's go and check*
DAISY: *He's in the mud*
ME: *What have you found George … George* (George is running away from me)
GEORGE: *He wants to go on my pic…*
ME: *Look at him!*
MILO: *Put wormy back!*
ME: *Wonderful*
MILO: *Don't hurt him!* (whine, high pitched)
GEORGE: *I'm not, he wants to go sticky on my picture*
MILO: *Don't stick him on there!* (whine, high pitched)
ME: *What about on the mud…Oh dear I hope that didn't hurt him… he dropped, fell a long way didn't he?*

FIGURE 7.1 'George found a worm'.
Photo authors own.

FIGURE 7.2 'He wants to go sticky on my picture.'
Photo authors own.

Daisy seemed quick to draw my attention to George's find; there was concern in her voice as if she was asking me to intervene as an authority that could put things right. Indeed, I responded immediately to her request, or maybe as a consequence of my own fears; like the children I was aware that George had a history with worms, and perhaps I did not want to be implicated in another 'worm death'. Milo, too, appeared quick to join me in this endeavour. I wondered whether he doubted my ability to fulfil his perception of justice, as one who was also positioned as carer of the child. It followed that in the duty of dispensing justice, Milo and I seem to have had differing approaches. In my case I sought to persuade George to my way of thinking, of seeing the worm as a sentient being. Perhaps that was why I took up his gendering of the worm as 'he', whereas in another situation I might have challenged this; use of the pronoun 'he' enabled me to enter into the action, implying the worm was a boy, like George, thus relying on him seeing the worm as sentient like himself. Milo also seemed driven by a conceptualisation of the worm as sentient but he was more direct, ordering George to do what he perceived as the 'right' thing. I am sure orders from me would have been rejected. George seemed determined to stick the worm to his picture which suggests that he perceived the worm as having value in this community that would give him status represented in this way in his art. He had misjudged the way in which his community would receive this.

GEORGE: *Where I shall I put him on mud, well I shall put him on land.*
ME: *Oh, ow*, [worm falls] … *oh* [inaudible said under breath]
GEORGE: [laughing]

ME: *Maybe George…*
MILO: *Mummy, I need some string*
ME: *…maybe if put some mud here, he wouldn't have so far to fall…shall we stick a bit of mud on there*
GEORGE: *Where's wormy wormy* [whining]
ME: *You don't want him to be hurt do you, he's very important to us*
GEORGE: *I'll put him in here… I'll make him a nice home* [loudly]
ME: *I think that's a good solution*

George's subsequent response to our intra-actions seems positive, leading me to ponder about what worked. My approach espouses Siraj-Blatchford et al.'s (2008) conceptualisation of Sustained Shared Thinking (SST). This focuses on the practitioner engaging in thinking or action with a child to prolong and improve a learning experience. In my own sense-making I realise that my knowledge of SST is underpinned by awareness of Vygotsky's (McLeod, 2020) 'Zone of Proximal Development' (ZPD) and the idea of the 'More Knowledgeable Other' (MKO). McLeod (2020) suggests that the most effective MKO is a slightly older peer, hence George may have been more willing to accept directions from Milo, as opposed to myself, with a particular adult power position. I reflect that my suggestion of a mud platform near the bottom of the canvas had been an attempt to intervene in a situation that appeared to be escalating beyond my capacities and to bring about the 'justice' that other children involved might be expecting. I felt relieved when George decided to make a home for the worm, and again I sense that I drew upon my practitioner educator experience, by adopting Bandura's theory of positive reinforcement (McLeod, 2016). I therefore praised George for his solution.

The victim:
For the worm, 'he' is perhaps neither he nor she, as worms are hermaphroditic. It was possible to point out this scientific fact during our intra-actions, and, as an ECP, on many occasions I do. Yet at other times, like today, I choose to put the 'he' worm before science. Similarly I frequently find myself wondering with children as to whether it hurts a worm when it drops from a height. After all worms make no audible sounds to indicate that they are in pain. Yet, I know from Zirbes et al. (2010) that worms are sentient as they are thigmotactic, responding to touch and seeking contact with other worms; whilst Hoskins (2019) from the Woodland Trust website points out that nerves in a worm's skin send messages to its brain 'controlling how it feels and moves'. Thus, a worm might feel pain as well as other emotions. The vibrations of rain on soil draw worms to the surface (earthwormsoc, n.d.). I wonder about the worm wriggling in George's hands; does it respond to his touch; as its head probes the air, is it reaching for the source of his vibrating voice? Perhaps a form of communication is taking place between George and the worm, because George seems to respond sensitively.

GEORGE: *Nice home wormy, wormy you got a nice home, wormy you got a nice home ahh… wormy where do you wanna come wormy* [with loud voice] *Ahh… aaa* [inaudible] *love you wormy* [with soft voice].

Nurturing nature with(in) children (or 'George killed the worm') **79**

FIGURE 7.3 'I'll make him a nice home'.

FIGURE 7.4 'Wormy' in his home'.

The intra-action concludes with George making the worm a home in the ground and his chatter with the worm reminds me of role-play. James and James (2011, p. 99) suggest that children's play 'is a key context for the process of interpretive reproduction – that which enables children to learn about the social world'. Perhaps viewed through the lens of role-play, the worm becomes a social actor and George and the worm are constructing knowledge together. Hence, the value of the worm appears to shift from the object of art-making where 'he' was *'sticky on my picture'*, to a 'being' capable of demanding and reciprocating affection: *'love you, wormy'* (said George). I am reminded in this instance, of post-humanist feminist Haraway's (2016) concept of 'companion species' whereby humans and animals might act as equals in a shared world.

The following intra-action suggests that any change in George's attitude to the worm was short-lived. A few minutes after his role-play attachment, Isabella announced that, *'George has killed the worm'*. I found myself returning to my role of judge (and jury). On questioning George, he claimed that *'wormy'* had *'digged his hole'*. At this point Milo arrived on the scene to accuse George of having pulled the worm apart. I asked George where he had put the worm, as there remained a possibility that we might be able to take *'him to worm hospital'*. George answered that he had *'putted him in worm hospital'*, though on further interrogation '[he didn't] *know where'* hospital was. Yet, he led me to a spot close by ('hospital' perhaps) and said: *'Let me just check … no I didn't see any worm'*. I hereby seem to pass judgement on the worm's death:

ME: *next time you find a worm … do you think you could … take a bit more care of him … because worms are very important to us, do you know why?*
GEORGE: *No*
ME: *Why do you think worms might be important to us … what do they do?*
GEORGE: *I don't know*
ME: *Well worms eat all the thing[s] on the ground, leaves and stuff to make mud and then we grow our food in the mud … do you like bread?*
GEORGE: *Yeah*
ME: *Do you like pizza?*
GEORGE: *Yeah*
ME: *Well if worms didn't do their job we wouldn't get pizza … or bread … or lots of other things, so that's why it's very important that we take care of worms. Do you think George next time you could take more care of the worm?*
GEORGE: *Yeah*
ME: *Okay, thank you.*

Once again, George's view of the worm appears to alter. On this occasion the worm's death by 'dismemberment' became, perhaps prompted by me, a worm worth saving by a dash to hospital. I am led to wonder whether George's seemingly alternating views of the worm from object of play to sentient being are related to Vygotskian social learning theory alone or whether there might be another intra-actively engaged force at work. To this end, I am reminded of Davies's (2014b, p. 737) explanation of social exclusion anxiety as an emotion that 'drives everyone to find ways to ensure their own continuing inclusion – in effect, their own existence as social beings'. I wonder whether George's fascination with worms and his ability to adapt are prompted by a desire to be more like children in this group who care for worms, and are subsequently praised by me for their good conforming conduct.

Hoskins (2019) explains that worms can regenerate. Whether, or not, this happens depends on the cut. If the head end retains the vital organs, there is a possibility of survival. Faced with near-death worm dilemmas in the ECEC setting, I introduce the notion of worm hospital, a place of hope perhaps, where, in terms of evolution and the worm's ability to regenerate as a survival strategy, accidents might be righted. As I see it, earthworms are pizza makers: they are fundamental to the food chain. On one-hand they are tasty food for blackbirds and hedgehogs, and on the other, they are decomposers that release nutrients into the soil from materials viewed by humans as immaterial or resourceless. In terms of our human survival we need worms to grow food, to eat and survive, hence taking care of worms is fundamental to notions of sustainability.

The police:

GEORGE: *I'm gonna see if I can get worms again … I might find more wormy*
ME: *George if you find a worm…*
GEORGE: *Don't kill it*
ME: *Yeah, please take care of it*
GEORGE: *Yeah, I know*
ME: *It needs to stay in one piece and alive*
ISABELLA: *And I also saw George doing this with his old wormy… swinging it around*
ME: *Hmm, what do you think will happen to the poor old worm if it gets swung around?*
ISABELLA: *dropped and stepped on …. and killed*
ME: *Yeah, I think after all that it would be hard to be alive, could you imagine if you'd been swung around, dropped from a height and then stepped on, I certainly wouldn't want that to happen to me.*

Looking back, I wondered whether I was motivated by a Vygotskian desire that George should over-hear and learn from his peer Isabella, or whether it was a strategy to reassure Isabella that I take worm 'atrocities' seriously. However, now it occurs to me that Isabella was perhaps policing both me and George: reminding me of the ethic I must enforce, and letting George know that she holds him accountable to some idea of a 'higher authority'. Shortly after this intra-action, Isabella appears to deploy the junk model python she had been making on George, rather in the manner of a police dog.

ISABELLA: *So we need a little bit of string to hold on there…Watch it George there's a python here might bite you if you be a little bit too annoying*
GEORGE: *Is that a py… PY/thon*

This exchange between Isabella and George reminds me of Davies's (2006, p 425) explanation of 'subjectification' as a process that shapes 'how we become who we are, and what we are'. Here, George seems to accept Isabella's policing by engaging with her fantasy, whilst, at the same time resisting her total control of him in his wording and voicing of the word py…PY/thon. Perhaps collective policing and monitoring of George paid off eventually. In a final worm intra-action, George arrived by my side tenderly cupping *"Baby wormy"*:

GEORGE: *Baby wormy* (in background) … *I love you baby wormy… I love baby wormy, I* [inaudible] *you baby wormy, mmm…* (moving towards me then stopping by my side)
ME: *Hello baby wormy, are you ok baby wormy? Did you pull..? Did you pull baby wormy out the ground?*
GEORGE: *No, I, I, yeah*
ME: *Okay, I think that might be half a baby wormy*
GEORGE: *No*
ME: *No… when you pull, get wormy out the ground can you use something to dig him out, so you don't break him… I think you might have half a wormy there*
GEORGE: *I think I, you, lost his tail*
ME: *I think he's lost his tail*
ISABELLA: *I think he's lost his tail*
ME: *If he's lucky… that…* (George runs off)

Perhaps by assenting to the notion of the 'lost tail' I was able – in some way – to engage with Haraway's (2016) concept of 'response-ability' for the planet and all organisms on it. Response-ability is about recognising that we live in the present and engaging in "a praxis of care and response" with other species for the benefit of the whole planet (ibid., 2016, p. 105). At the same time, I wanted to avoid discouraging George from engaging in 'worm care' in the ways other children seem to have taken on board and responded to. Davies's (2014a) explanation of social exclusion anxiety suggests that George's intra-actions might have been about conforming to a way of being included with this group of children that he socialises with outside the research context (which also involves me on occasions). George ran away before I'd had time to complete my sentence, he was soon apprehended at a water bucket, by Milo.

MILO: *Mummy, I managed to save the worm he was about to drown the worm*
ME: *I think that was half a worm, maybe, do you think you could put it into a worm hospital Milo*

This sequence of worm intra-actions concluded with my asking Milo, my MKO, to do the 'right thing' by the worm, in the hope that perhaps he would be witnessed by George and the other children around who demanded justice for worms. Yet, reflecting on George at the water bucket I now wonder whether George was perhaps engaged in a ritual for dealing with a hurt or dead worm which involved washing it clean. Reflecting on this story I recognise how I made conscious decisions that drew on my ECP knowledge. For example, I utilised the children's MKO potential to deploy them in the manner of police agents to establish the justice they expected and to bring George into line with their values, which were in turn shaped by me. In this sense the children positioned me as the judge, a higher authority, perhaps appealing to my post-humanist sensibilities for other species, of which our shared pedagogical histories would have made them aware. In the research arena my educator knowledge worked as a tool to negotiate the complexities of being a judge, a carer of children and someone who has a particular post-humanist view that advocates for inter-species justice.

Conclusion

The story of George and the worms reveals the existence of a moral code within this small community that I conceptualise as an ethic of 'interspecies justice'. In the analysis I sought to highlight how, as a community seeking to include other species, the children and I took up positions of judge, jury, police, victim and an individual who must learn the code so that the status quo might be maintained. The analysis reveals how this group of children engaged with ethical notions of right and wrong, and collective political activism, to bring about justice for the worms involved, illustrating how moral codes evolve from communities (Christians, 2018). Congruent with a post-humanist perspective, children seemed able to consider the perspectives of other species and thereby demonstrated compassion and responsibility for more-than-humans.

The story also highlights ways in which ECPs' knowledge and pedagogies constantly shape, inform and become reshaped and re-formed through encounters with nature. At the interface of children, nature, and sustainability the analysis provoked by the interpretive process suggests that ECPs are constantly called upon to make momentary ethical judgements arising from multiple sources. On the one-hand these may be influenced by community desires for the nurturing of sustainable citizens, and on the other, they might be shaped by personal values, knowledge and experience. ECP's ethical decisions and their consequences are, therefore, part and parcel of practice. Such a way of being and practising demands a sophisticated level of dynamic sensibility, skill and responsibility. As Ärlemalm-Hagsér and Elliott (2017) suggest, ECPs' values have potential to shape setting practices and children's thinking and responses in relation to nature and sustainability, just as they do in so many other areas of the young child's life. ECPs shoulder a significant responsibility.

This single research story of 'George and the Worms' indicates that children's daily intra-actions with other species, taking place in the micro context of ECEC, are linked to how they construct their ideas about nature; this matters in terms of the wider macro context of a world in need of sustainability. It is encouraging that the new *Development Matters* (DfE, 2021, p. 61) suggests supporting children in 'the careful handling of a worm and helping children to return it to the dug-up soil'. The aim of wider research from which this chapter is drawn is to contribute to ECEC guidance by revealing why care for other species is important for children and communities (beyond notions of children's individual learning and development), as well as how shared ethics of sustainability may emerge in small communities that include children, worms and dynamic, sensitive and skilled ECPs positioned as child 'nature' nurturers.

> **REFLECTIVE POINTS**
>
> Reflect on your outdoor practice or occasions where you spend time with children in nature:
>
> - What are the species that share your environment?
> - How do you feel about them?
> - How do the children react to them?
>
> How do you, or might you bring children and these species together so that they may come to know one another as what Haraway (2016) describes as 'companion species'?

References

Ärlemalm-Hagsér, E. and Elliott, S. (2017). Special issue: contemporary research on early childhood education for sustainability. *International Journal Early Childhood*, 49(3), pp. 267–272.

Bailey, K. (2019). 'Nature as 'good' an ECEC product and practice', *TACTYC: Association for Professional Development in Early Years*. Available at: https://tactyc.org.uk/reflections/ (Accessed 22 October 2019).

Bento, G. and Dias, G. (2017). The importance of outdoor play for young children's healthy development. *Porto Biomedical Journal*, 2(5), pp. 157–160.

Biesta, G.J.J. (2016). *The Beautiful Risk of Education*. Oxon: Routledge.

Blaise, M., Hamm, C. and Iorio, J.M. (2017). Modest witness(ing) and lively stories: paying attention to matters of concern in early childhood. *Pedagogy, Culture & Society*, 25(1), pp. 31–42.

Coles, J. (2016) 'How Nature is Good for our Health and Happiness', BBC Earth, 20 April. Available at: http://www.bbc.com/earth/story/20160420-how-nature-is-good-for-our-health-and-happiness (Accessed 5 July 2019).

Chawla, L. (2015). Benefits of nature contact for children. *Journal of Planning Literature*, 30(4), pp. 433–452.

Christians, C.G. (2018). Ethics and politics in qualitative research, in Denzin, N.K. and Lincoln, Y.S. (eds.), *Handbook of Qualitative Research* (5th ed.). London: SAGE Publications Ltd, pp. 66–82. *Kortext* [e-book reader]. Available at: https://app.kortext.com/epub/253527 (Accessed 25 May 2020).

Davies, B. (2006). Subjectification: the relevance of Butler's analysis for education. *British Journal of Sociology of Education*, 27(4) pp. 425–438.

Davies, B. (2014a). Reading anger in early childhood intra-actions: a diffractive analysis. *Qualitative Inquiry*, 20(6), pp. 734–741. doi: 10.1177/1077800414530256

Davies, B. (2014b). *Listening to children: being and becoming*. Oxon: Routledge.

Department of Education. (2021). *Development matters; Non statutory guidance for the early years foundation stage*. Available at: https://assets.publishing.service.gov.uk/government/uploads/system/uploads/attachment_data/file/988004/Development_Matters.pdf (Accessed 9 July 2021).

Earthworm Society. (n.d.). Why do earthworms come out when it rains? [WWW Document]. Available at: https://www.earthwormsoc.org.uk/FAQrain (Accessed 23 September 2021).

Guha, R. (2006). *How much should a person consume? Environmentalism in India and the United States*. London: University of California Press.

Haraway, D.J. (2016). *Staying with the trouble: making Kin in the Chthulucene*. Durham, NC and London: Duke University Press.

Haughton, C. and Ellis, C. (2016). Play, in Palaiologou, I. (ed.), *The early years foundation stage; theory and practice*. London: SAGE publications Ltd, pp. 130–147.

Hinds. (2019). Education experts say children are reaping the benefits of boom in early-learning centres held in countryside and parks, *The Sunday Post*, 29 July. Available at: https://www.sundaypost.com/fp/education-experts-say-children-reaping-the-benefits-of-boom-in-early-learning-centres-held-in-countryside-and-parksruaridhs-storyitslovely-to-hear-him-come-home-and-ta/ (Accessed 15 October 2019).

Hoskins. (2019). Do worms have eyes? And other worm facts [WWW Document]. *Woodland Trust*. Available at: https://www.woodlandtrust.org.uk/blog/2019/04/do-worms-have-eyes/ (Accessed 2 February 2021).

James, A., James, A. (2011) *Key concepts in childhood studies* London: SAGE Publications Ltd.

Louv, R. (2010). *Last child in the woods: saving our children from nature-deficit disorder*. London: Atlantic Books.

Louv, R.(2016). *Vitamin N; The essential guide to a nature-rich life*. North Carolina: Algonquin Books of Chapel Hill.

Lyndon, S.J. (2019) *Early years practitioners' narratives of poverty in early childhood*. Doctoral thesis (EdD), University of Sussex.

Magee, A. (2017) 'Why fresh air is the best medicine', *The Telegraph*. 16 August. Available at: https://www.telegraph.co.uk/health-fitness/body/why-fresh-air-is-the-best-medicine/ (Accessed 4 July 2019).

Maller, C.J. (2009). Promoting children's mental, emotional and social health through contact with nature: a model. *Health Education*, 109(6), pp. 522–543.

McLeod, S.A. (2016). Bandura - social learning theory. *Simply Psychology*. Available at: www.simplypsychology.org/bandura.html (Accessed 6 February 2022).

McLeod, S.A. (2020). Lev Vygotsky's sociocultural theory. *Simple Psychology*. Available at: https://www.simplypsychology.org/vygotsky.html (Accessed 2 May 2021).

McLeod, N. and Giardiello, P. (2019). *Empowering early childhood educators: international pedagogies as provocation*. Oxon: Routledge.

Siraj-Blatchford, I., Taggart, B., Sylva, K., Sammons, P. and Melhuish, E. (2008). Towards the transformation of practice in early childhood education: the effective provision of pre-school education (EPPE) project. *Cambridge Journal of Education*, 38(1), pp. 23–36.

Taylor, A. (2013). *Reconfiguring the natures of childhood*. Oxon: Routledge.

Taylor, A. and Giugni, M. (2012). Common worlds: reconceptualising inclusion in early childhood communities. *Contemporary Issues in Early Childhood*, 13(2), pp. 108–119. doi: 10.2304/ciec.2012.13.2.108

Taylor, A. and Pacini-Ketchabaw, V. (2015). Learning with children, ants, and worms in the anthropocene: towards a common world pedagogy of multispecies vulnerability. *Pedagogy, Culture and Society*, 23(4), pp. 507–529.

van Dooren, T. (2016). *Flight ways: life and loss at the edge of extinction*. Chichester: Columbia University Press.

Weldemariam, K., Boyd, D., Hirst, N., Sageidet, B.M., Browder, J.K., Grogan, L. and Hughes, F. (2017). *International Journal of Early Childhood*, 49(3), pp. 333–351

Zirbes, L., Deneubourg, J.-L., Brostaux, Y. and Haubruge, E. (2010). A new case of consensual decision: collective movement in earthworms. *Ethology*, 116, pp. 546–553. doi: 10.1111/j.1439-0310.2010.01768.x

8
EMBRACING CREATIVITY IN THE EARLY YEARS

Jacqueline Young

Introduction

Over recent decades creativity has been included as an important aim of UK EC curriculums, regardless of the political leanings of the government in power. Creativity is a curriculum area that is found in all four UK EC curriculums (The Scottish Government, 2008; Wales and Department for Children, 2015; Council for the Curriculum, Examinations and Assessment, 2018; DfE, 2021); with the Statutory Framework for the Early Years Foundation Stage in England (DfE, 2021, p. 21), adding 'creating and thinking critically - children have and develop their own ideas, make links between ideas, and develop strategies for doing things' as one of the three characteristics of effective learning that practitioners *must* reflect on and incorporate into their planning when working with young children.

Definitions of creativity

The question of what creativity actually is (similar to the quality debate) is a difficult one to answer. Discussions around the nature of creativity in general can be complex and no agreement has yet been reached on a precise definition. Historically, creativity has been investigated from a wide range of perspectives, and, as a result, the definition of what it is and how it can be nurtured has become increasingly complex and varied. In fact, there have been so many different definitions of creativity over the years that some writers have striven to categorise these definitions into types. For instance, Fleith (2000, p. 148) proposes that concepts of creativity can be broadly categorised into four groups: 'person, product, process and the environment'. Such categorisation of creativity matters, as, depending on the perspective taken, creativity could either be related to innate abilities, dependent on

DOI: 10.4324/9781003206262-9

the product or outcome, inherent in a process or way of working, or influenced by external factors (such as educational, social and cultural contexts).

When it comes to applying concepts of creativity to educational contexts, the 1999 National Advisory Committee for Creative and Cultural Education (NACCCE) report, *All Our Futures*, gives a useful definition of creativity as 'Imaginative activity fashioned so as to produce outcomes that are both original and of value' (NACCCE, 1999, p. 930). This definition relies on two key underpinning premises: first, that everyone has the capacity to be creative (Lin, 2011), and second, that creativity can be developed (ibid.). The idea that creativity is a 'universal capacity' (Siraj-Blachford, 2007, p. 7) implies that all children have the capacity to both demonstrate and develop creativity and creative thinking skills. This is important as it then follows that creativity can be taught and nurtured or constrained and limited.

Prentice (2000) suggests that a common thread through many definitions of creativity is the need for novelty or originality. Recently, there has been a growing recognition that creativity can be seen beyond the traditional arts-based subjects and across all curriculum areas, including science. Robson (2014, p. 122) further clarifies concepts of originality as ideas that are 'new for that individual, not necessarily for society as a whole', building on ideas of novelty in relation to creativity. This idea that everyone can be creative and that originality can be more broadly interpreted is linked to the conclusion that creativity is 'visible across the broadest range of everyday contexts in daily life' (Robson, 2014, p. 122). Craft (2001, p. 2) dubbed this type of creativity 'little c creativity' and defined it as 'everyday, life wide creativity'. This definition of creativity seems particularly pertinent to the kind of creative acts that might be observed in the play of young children, and so seems most relevant to ideas of creativity encapsulated in this chapter.

Fisher (2004) identified that many writers differentiate between two kinds of thinking when describing the processes related to creativity: creative thinking and critical thinking. In contrast, the report *All Our Futures* (NACCCE, 1999) supports the idea that critical thinking *is an aspect of* creative thinking and not separate. The NACCCE report states that 'Evaluating which ideas do work and which do not requires judgement and criticism. In this way, creative thinking always involves some critical thinking' (NACCCE, 1999, p. 33). This would suggest that any observable enactment of creative thinking would also contain observable elements of critical thinking.

Craft (2001), Jeffrey and Craft (2004) and Burnard et al. (2006) suggest that one possible approach for supporting children's creative thinking is possibility thinking. Burnard et al. characterise possibility thinking as: 'posing questions, play, immersion, innovation, risk taking, being imaginative and self-determination' (Burnard et al., 2006, p. 257), whilst they characterise effective learning as: 'creating and thinking critically'. In the English *Early Years Curriculum Framework*, these concepts are interpreted as 'children have and develop their own ideas, make links between ideas, and develop strategies for doing things' (DfE, 2021, p. 16). This wording noticeably does not reference risk or play, which, it could be argued, are two elements which provide some sense of 'how', when considering ways that creative thinking, and creativity might be supported.

What are creative pedagogies?

The NACCCE (1999, p. 89) defines teaching creatively as 'using imaginative approaches to make learning more interesting and effective' and defines teaching for creativity as teaching that is intended to develop the creative thinking or actions of the learner themselves. Jeffrey and Craft (2004, p. 84) suggest that creative teaching and teaching for creativity cannot be easily separated and that 'The former is inherent in the latter and the former often leads directly to the latter'. They argue that the degree to which a teacher embraces creativity in their own teaching acts as a strong model for pupils, even if the teacher's original intention was not to teach creativity. Lin (2011) suggests a model of 'creative pedagogy' where the three elements of creative teaching, teaching for creativity and creative learning (of the learner/pupil or child) are interconnected and interrelated. This implies that teachers who are themselves more creative and employ creative approaches in their teaching are better at fostering creative abilities in children than teachers who teach in a more rigid traditional style.

Although they do not directly reference their ideas as creative pedagogy, Burnard et al. (2006) describe how creative teaching and creative learning in ECEC foster the development of possibility thinking as an aspect of creativity. Their model features both creative learning and creative teaching, but also introduces a third factor, the enabling context. This is important, as it suggests that context may be a key influencer when it comes to creative pedagogies, in direct contrast to Lin's (2011) model where context is not mentioned at all.

A brief overview of the research approach

The rest of this chapter consists of an analysis of a reflective discussion between two Early Childhood Practitioners (ECPs), Lily and Astrid, about how creativity is supported in early years' settings. The discussion involved two student practitioners who had recently been awarded Early Years Teacher Status. To stimulate discussion, I shared ten images generated by Google using the search term 'creative learning Early Years' with them, asking them to comment on any of the images provided, with no preset agenda or interview plan.

Definitions and understandings of creativity

When looking through the initial stimulus pictures, Astrid wanted to discuss that some of the stimulus pictures contained images beyond the traditional arts-based subjects.

> You know, I like that there was a picture of you know, clearly maths and science and they should be, in my opinion, equally, you know, creative as something like paint and chalk.

Astrid appeared to agree with this wider construction of creativity, but when discussing whether process or product are important when it comes to creative activity, Astrid suggested that the two are far harder to separate than the literature might lead us to expect:

> A lot of the stuff that ended up in the bin at nursery … for me, even though I think the process is really important, I still think that show respect for that piece of artwork they've made somehow or returned to it another day or display it in some way, or it was sad when it literally got no recognition. They didn't even speak about it or what had happened or so it was like the process hadn't really been acknowledged. So perhaps process lost value because of that.

Both ECPs associated the idea of risk with concepts of creative development. For example, Astrid commented that 'You've got to take risks to be creative. I think they're kind of two things that are linked,' and Lily remarked that:

> I think you don't want it to be kind of explicit of what they've got to do, you want to be able to, like make choices and within that, you know, to take risks, not to themselves, that maybe if things will work and that trial-and-error process.

Astrid connected this back to wider definitions of creativity and creative thinking, reflecting that: 'once you lay the foundations of … risk taking and celebrating that within a school, then I think it will feed out into all areas (in) the curriculum making everything richer'. She also considered how this might affect the provision, sharing: 'I think creativity is all about the unknown and the uncertain, and it's making children comfortable with that. And you could totally embed that in your provision'. This reflection is interesting, as it suggests that developing student ECPs own understandings of concepts of creativity might be essential, if positive working practices supporting the development of creativity are to be embedded.

Interestingly, the ECPs conceptualised the debate around whether creativity was learnt or innate as complex. For instance, Astrid asserted that 'I think maybe babies are more creative than reception', a comment undisputed by Lily. This would imply that these ECPs see creativity as something innate, something children are born with, and yet also something that might diminish over time if not nurtured or taught. Astrid suggested that modelling is essential if creativity is to thrive, explaining: 'I think a lot of children I've worked with … need some modelling of creative thinking from an adult or from their peers around them.' This idea seemed to be echoed by Lily, who went on to suggest that adult intervention is key in broadening these initial creative responses through broadening the creative opportunities they have access to.

The role of the adult

The subject of the role of the adult in supporting creativity and creative thinking came up repeatedly. Lily argued that the adult's role is to manage resources, to reduce and channel the creative possibilities:

> at my setting they had, they always had a making table, always been like boxes and recycling stuff they could model with, and often a lot of the children would end up just really fascinated with the tape, and tape things, and tape things, and tape things. That meant we had to think about what kind of tape we put out, because then they weren't actually able to use it for the making, because they had to tape around themselves, instead of taping round boxes.

Astrid disagreed with this construction of the adult role and postulated the opposite view, that the adult's role is to open up possibilities and provide resources, not restrict access to materials, saying: 'I think as open, as open ended as you can be with stimulus and resources and ... provocation is, is when I've seen children be the most creative. This is interesting, as although both ECPs seem in agreement that adult intervention matters, the discussion between the two ECPs could be read as exemplifying the tensions that these recently qualified practitioners feel between providing opportunities to play and explore materials and techniques and feeling a pressure to manage perceived negative behaviours, or work towards a set outcome.

Lily raised the issue of her own confidence around creative activity impacting on what she might and might not provide in terms of support, commenting that 'I'd find it daunting if there were a load of resources, and you could do anything with them. You might be better at that sort of thing?'. Clearly the implication is that a practitioner with greater confidence in their own creative capacities may provide greater variation of resources and wider opportunities for children to express creativity. Therefore, the practitioner becomes key to the nurturing or narrowing of creativity in children.

The role of the learning environment

Both Lily and Astrid talked about how the environment can be just as important as the adults. Lily commented that:

> ... they can get a lot from an adult, they have been helping them but actually, a well-resourced and well set up and kind of well-constructed environment can do that for them, too. There's lots of opportunities within it.

The two ECPs shared anecdotes about their placement experiences, discussing how some settings limit access to certain resources, suggesting this affects children's confidence with those materials. However, Lily went on to also suggest an alternative view, that, when it comes to resourcing, sometimes less can also be more:

> I think kind of the flip side of it is you're if you're so, if you're working so hard to set up, you know, really strong continuous provision, where everything is set up as high quality with lots of things for them to do all the time, you then kind of lose, you could lose that kind of curiosity. So I think there's been talk, at my setting of just one day, just removing all the furniture from the room, and removing some of the toys and just filling the room with cardboard boxes, and kind of, you want to, you want to kind of challenge what the children ... So we can kind of bring a element of challenge and of disruption into that.

This suggests that too many physical resources may in fact restrict creative responses from children, as this may lead to ECPs suggesting what children should use and how. It intimates that a more minimalist approach to resourcing may open the creative capabilities of children as they imagine different ways that those few resources might be used. It could be argued that this is an oblique reference to the creativity of the adult planning and resourcing the setting; that the resources themselves are perhaps not as important as the vision of the adult providing the resources. Although Lily's statement seems to contradict earlier discussions around the impact of resourcing, it confirms that both ECPs recognise that how the environment is constructed can either enable or constrain the creative development of children in a setting. It also, perhaps, demonstrates that the environment is, in fact, constructed by the adults that work in it, and as such, adult influence goes way beyond actual child/adult interactions.

The role of policy and setting ethos

Referencing the influence of macro-scale policy on practice, Lily recognised that creative and critical thinking is woven into the English EC Framework, but suggested that this does not in fact mean that all settings interpret policy in the same way. Astrid agreed, highlighting her own experiences of settings having distinct approaches to acknowledging and supporting creative activity, despite drawing on the same policy frameworks:

> I found at nursery, ... it was less important, the end product. It was much more process lead. And then I felt a real flip in the reception class where it was more about the display at the end and making something pretty to take home.

Astrid reflected on how the inclusion of creative and critical thinking in key early years policy has raised the profile of creativity in early years settings, but that this hasn't always followed through into setting pedagogies and practice:

> I think creative thinking is talked a lot more about now. It's kind of it was like, I think people acknowledge that it's … that the child we are educating in this world, that we're not sure why it's going to be … that that creative, sort of innovative thinking is like crucial. I think there's a lot of talk around that. But whether I see it played out in practice, in my setting, I'm not sure. It's still very much rote learning.

Lily agreed, discussing how her setting reacted to her planning for characteristics of effective learning, such as creative and critical thinking, as part of her training course:

> It was so far removed from their practice that me, me coming in and having to link my evidence to that was quite, even for my mentor, was a bit like, 'Oh!'. It was hard for them to, … get their head round it. That it was so important.

On the topic of how different settings value creative activity, Astrid noted that schools are under pressure to perform in certain curriculum areas, and that means that creative activity is sometimes pushed out of the curriculum, suggesting that 'when the class is under pressure to meet other targets or to do anything else. It's the first thing that's kind of not delivered that week'.

Lily and Astrid both agreed that what work settings choose to display often signalled what is and is not valued, setting the tone for practitioners in terms of what curriculum priorities are set. Lily commented that:

> Maths and their attempts at mark making and writing end up on a wall, but actually their painting or their acting out of stories, all these creative processes, aren't acknowledged or captured somehow.

Lily went on to suggest that how settings plan and generate curriculum can either enhance or restrict opportunities for creative activity:

> they did a lot of their sort of termly planning on a two-year rolling kind of stuff. They were repeating things, but they're not repeating things for children, that would stay more than a year. But actually, they weren't kind of breaking away from it. There was the same book, there was kind of … they have resources from 15, 20 years ago, they were still using. Which is obviously great, but you're not kind of thinking beyond that.

Lily commented that even the contextual issue of the physical space available at settings impacts on resource organisation, and therefore how creativity might be supported, explaining: *'because they kind of were limited by their space, and there were kind of other limitations, they kind of had to be more creative in what they were doing'*.

The impact of children's personal contexts and prior knowledge

The topic of how children's individual contexts and prior experiences impact on their engagement with creative activity came up several times. Astrid suggested that children who have had less experience with traditional creative materials might need more adult support and scaffolding to access certain materials in the setting:

> Sometimes that thing of not knowing where to stop with something we're doing. I noticed some of the children just didn't know when, so it is keep printing, keep printing on top until it just became this sort of muddy mess. And actually, those children that were a bit more adept at that sort of creative process can see it a bit more aesthetically and knew when it had filled up the space now and it wasn't that kind of need to go and keep going. It was self-regulated a lot better, which is perhaps part of the creative process.

Astrid went on to make a link between children from backgrounds of social disadvantage and a lack of experience with certain materials and experiences, postulating that this in turn can lead to poor development of creativity:

> I found that, because my school is high percentage of PP [Pupil Premium] … I really noticed a difference, with their ability to think creatively. With the children that were disadvantaged, I just didn't think they were … they either approached it by just almost, just throwing themselves in it, and it became very messy. Could … like just completely unstructured, because they didn't have access to it usually … (or) they didn't approach it at all because it was so foreign to them. That actually, they went and played with the balls or something, something they knew. Whereas, the children that were clearly used to it were experimenting in interesting ways with sort of taking their time with things were definitely slower and more questioning about things, testing out resources in different ways. You could sense the real creative process that they were sort of comfortable with, whereas, the others, it was it was very sensory. And then they were just sort of throwing themselves at the paint …

Lily picked this up and went further, controversially linking disadvantage and lack of experience with creative materials to extreme risk taking, **'Yeah, I think it's this like extreme of risk. I think sometimes disadvantaged children might be the ones that are kind of always pushing, always pushing boundaries'**. Astrid appeared to agree with this construction, nodding as Lily spoke.

Discussion

The literature section of this chapter briefly explored the wider debate around definitions of creativity, but what is clear from the ECPs' discussion is that both accept that very young children are capable of creativity and that their own actions impact on this; even if the mechanism by which this occurs is less clear for them. Lily's reference to her lack of confidence in her own creative capacities and how that might impact on her own pedagogical choices would seem to lend weight to the ideas of Lin (2011), that the creative confidence of adults supporting creative learning is important. One possible implication for this on the training of ECPs is that much more time and effort may need to be put in during training to support a developing ECP's own creative confidence and competence.

The construction suggested by Lily that disadvantaged children can be extreme risk takers with poorly developed creative skills, seems at odds with Burnard et al.'s (2006) conceptualisation of risk taking as an inherent feature of possibility thinking, which is in turn presented as an aspect of creative thinking. Perhaps Lily's view reflects our narrowly defined views of what creativity 'looks like' and a reluctance to recognise more extreme behaviours (for example, painting or taping the self rather than inanimate objects) as 'creativity', so, instead, labelling them risk.

Earlier extracts of the discussion touch on the tensions ECPs feel between providing opportunities to explore and managing behaviour; and the construction of disadvantaged children presented in this discussion may well be another echo of this tension. It is, perhaps, unsurprising that the English EC curriculum makes no mention of risk in relation to supporting 'creating and critical thinking' (DfE, 2021, p. 16), whilst the Ofsted Inspection Framework by which English ECEC settings are appraised makes mention of the specific area of 'behaviour and attitudes' (Ofsted, 2019). Whilst both ECPs valued risk as an important part of creative development, what constitutes acceptable risk seemed both unclear to them as individuals and inconsistent across different settings.

Conclusion

Discussions about what is valued as an educational outcome, and what isn't, and how these values impact on practice, arose throughout this discussion. If a piece of writing is put up on the wall, but creative endeavours are put in the bin, what does this tell children about how practitioners are valuing the different learning? Although this is a very small-scale qualitative study, the themes identified in this chapter would suggest that more research around the impact of contextual factors may be needed to fully understand how context impacts on ECPs attitudes and conceptualisations, and how this in turn impacts on the pedagogical choices ECPs make, and how these pedagogical choices impact on the development of children's creativity.

The emphasis on context that comes through from the five key themes identified above supports the ideas of Burnard et al. (2006), that contextual factors have a strong influence on creative teaching and learning. This would suggest that settings wishing to be even better at supporting creative teaching and learning may benefit from adopting a reflective approach, considering their individual contextual influences. The themes identified here provide a useful, loose framework for such reflections, to support ECPs to think through how creativity is supported and developed, and to encourage them to consider their own positioning and identity as they support the creative development of children.

> **REFLECTIVE POINTS**
>
> Use the prompt points below to consider how your own practice and the practice in your setting might support creativity and creative development of young children:
>
> - Does your setting value process or product more and how is this value demonstrated in the setting?
> - How confident do you feel in your own creative skills? How might your skills affect your ability to support creativity in the children in your care?
> - What opportunities are there in your setting environment for children to express themselves creatively?
> - How is (or is?) creativity and creative thinking planned into your curriculum?
>
> What prior experiences do you think might influence how the children in your care engage with creativity?

References

Burnard, P. et al. (2006) 'Documenting "possibility thinking": a journey of collaborative enquiry', *International Journal of Early Years Education*, 14(3), pp. 243–262. doi:10.1080/09669760600880001.

Council for the Curriculum, Examinations and Assessment (2018) 'Curricular Guidance for Pre-School Education', Northern Ireland Department of Education. Available at: https://www.education-ni.gov.uk/sites/default/files/publications/education/PreSchool_Guidance_30May18_Web.pdf (Accessed 19 June 2021).

Craft, A. (2001) 'Little c creativity', in Jeffrey, B., Leibling, M., and Craft, A. (eds.) *Creativity in Education*. London and New York: Continuum, pp. 45–61.

DfE (2021) 'Statutory framework for the early years foundation stage Setting the standards for learning, development and care for children from birth to five', Department for Education. Available at: https://assets.publishing.service.gov.uk/government/uploads/system/uploads/attachment_data/file/974907/EYFS_framework_-_March_2021.pdf.

Fisher, R. (2004) 'What is creativity?' in Fisher, R and, Williams M. (Ed) *Unlocking creativity: teaching across the curriculum*. London, Routledge pp. 6–20.

de Fleith, D. S. (2000) 'Teacher and student perceptions of creativity in the classroom environment', *Roeper Review*, 22(3), pp. 148–153. doi:10.1080/02783190009554022.

Jeffrey, B. and Craft, A. (2004) 'Teaching creatively and teaching for creativity: distinctions and relationships', *Educational Studies*, 30(1), pp. 77–87. doi:10.1080/0305569032000159750.

Lin, Y.-S. (2011) 'Fostering creativity through education – a conceptual framework of creative pedagogy', *Creative Education*, 2(3), pp. 149–155. doi:10.4236/ce.2011.23021.

NACCCE (1999) *All our futures: creativity, culture and education*. London, DfEE. Available at: http://sirkenrobinson.com/pdf/allourfutures.pdf (Accessed 3 May 2019).

Ofsted (2019) 'Education inspection framework: overview of research' Manchester, Ofsted. Available at: chrome-extension://efaidnbmnnnibpcajpcglclefindmkaj/https://assets.publishing.service.gov.uk/government/uploads/system/uploads/attachment_data/file/963625/Research_for_EIF_framework_updated_references_22_Feb_2021.pdf (Accessed 18 July 2022).

Prentice, R. (2000) 'Creativity: a reaffirmation of its place in early childhood education', *The Curriculum Journal*, 11(2), pp. 145–158. doi:10.1080/09585170050045173.

Robson, S. (2014) 'The analysing children's creative thinking framework: development of an observation-led approach to identifying and analysing young children's creative thinking', *British Educational Research Journal*, 40(1), pp. 121–134. doi:10.1002/berj.3033.

Siraj-Blachford, I. (2007) 'Creativity, communication and collaboration: the identification of pedagogic progression in sustained shared thinking', *Asia-Pacific Journal of Research in early Childhood Education*, 1(2), pp. 2–23.

The Scottish Government (2008) *Scotland's curriculum for excellence, Scotland's curriculum for excellence*. Available at: http://scotlandscurriculum.scot/ (Accessed 19 June 2021).

Tims, C. (2010) *Born creative*. London: Demos.

Wales and Department for Children, E., Lifelong Learning and Skills (2015) *Curriculum for Wales foundation phase framework*. Cardiff. Available at: http://learning.gov.wales/docs/learningwales/publications/150803-fp-framework-en.pdf (Accessed 19 June 2021).

9
CHAMPIONING A *NOT KNOWING* PEDAGOGY AND PRACTICE

Rebecca Webb and Kathy Foster

Introduction

Transformation relates to processes of democratic engagement, inclusion and change in society (Biesta et al. 2010). Educationally, it involves democratising pedagogies that champion the voices and participation of preschool children, their families and practitioners to constitute a community (Malaguzzi, 1993; Murris, 2016). This chapter uses a case study of transformations in Green Shoots Community Nursery (our pseudonym), located in a town in Southern England. It draws upon voices of practitioners as they reflect on their role. The focus is on practitioner involvement and the significance of transformation for practitioner subjectivities (their sense of 'who they are' and 'who they might be', Biesta, 2009), as well as the evolving subjectivities of children in their charge (Davies, 2014). What emerges is the significance of a *not knowing* pedagogy, practice and care (Webb and Foster, 2020). *Not knowing* affords ethical and attentive commitment to ways of knowing, doing and being that foreground both practitioner and child in a constant process of 'becoming'.

Our context

Green Shoots, a privately owned nursery, opened ten years ago. Since then, there have been many changes in rethinking and repurposing the building and the outdoor space, as well as evolving policies and practices which challenge some of the dogmas of 'cultural conservatism' (Jones, 2013) inherent in English education systems. The number of children attending has grown and there have been several staff changes. There are also some constants: the manager has remained the same, and the longest serving practitioner has been at the setting for six years. The nursery has been recognised by Ofsted as 'outstanding' since opening.

DOI: 10.4324/9781003206262-10

The characteristics of Green Shoots have played a role in it gaining a respected reputation within the local community and beyond. Recently it has focused on becoming a pioneering, sustainable nursery, beginning with 'small steps' such as banishing single-use items and switching to reusable nappies. It has created a woodland garden to support multi-species biodiversity. Resources are open-ended, natural and recyclable 'loose parts' (Gibson et al., 2017), creating an environment for children to be inventive and creative in their own learning. Green Shoots' ethos attracts families who regard themselves as environmentally aware, those who wish their children to be exposed to the idea that they might 'make a difference' to society. Despite ambitions, such as UNESCO's *17 Sustainable Development Goals* (UNESCO, 2017) and some excellent resources, sustainability is not integral to *Early Childhood Education and Care* (ECEC) statutory guidance. Green Shoots sees itself as preparing the next generation with tools, dispositions and knowledge to safeguard an environmentally sustainable future.

When Green Shoots closed for extensive refurbishment, this provided opportunities for rethinking all aspects of practice and pedagogy. It reconsidered its value system and ideas around environment and nurture to refocus upon the dynamic of pedagogical moment-by-moment encounters with children. Its approach mirrored the newly configured ECEC sector-orchestrated *Birth to Five Matters* guidance (Early Years Coalition, 2021), which elevates the idea that settings can 'determine for themselves what, when, and how to offer the experiences and support to help children make progress in their learning and development' (ibid., p. 7). Green Shoots staggered the reintroduction of children with practitioners and children placed in vertically grouped 'family pods', challenging the orthodoxy of ECEC development discourse that children should be grouped in single-age categories.

Reading across literatures

Jacques Rancière (1991) provides a starting point for thinking about transformation and how to *be* in democratic communities in ways that *assume* our intellectual equality in order to live together. The ideas of Rancière (1991, p. 71) rest on the potential of all human beings within a society which repudiates 'the division between those who know, and those who don't'. Such ideas may run against the grain of the way many of us have been schooled, both formally and incidentally, through social assumptions of a world divided into: 'knowing minds and ignorant ones, ripe minds and immature ones, the capable and the incapable, the intelligent and the stupid' (ibid., p. 6). Institutional systems are predicated on the positivist idea that those with knowledge can enlighten those without. It assumes that there is always a Master Explainer (who knows) and an apprentice (who doesn't) and that, however much the apprentice learns, there remains a gap of inequality that reminds us of our incapacity.

We write this chapter in the context of current debates about re-framing the 'Early Years Foundation Phase' in England, where key government documents (namely the *Early Years Foundation Stage Statutory Framework*, 2021; and the non-statutory curriculum guidance, *Development Matters*, 2020) have recently been revised. Different perspectives rest on assumptions of democracy and equality; who has the right to be recognised as a 'knower' and in what context; the measuring and naming of 'gaps'; and the necessity to report on these. Such debates are a part of a consensus that requires, according to Rancière (2004), moments of transformation for democracy to happen. This transformation has nothing to do with how things ought to be organised in society but rather, democracy as a condition of change that finds meaning only when put in action. This presumes that equality is enacted through the very doing of something that enables human thriving, a moment which contains the possibility that 'learning surprises us; it takes us over, undoes our perspectives and radically changes our world views' (Dunne and Seery, 2016, p. 16). This notion of transformation as surprise that can undo and change is what we define as a *not knowing* ethos of pedagogy and practice (Webb and Foster, 2020). *Not knowing* is, therefore, about Rancièrian transformational pedagogy and practice that supports children in their curiosity, wonder and puzzlement.

Transformative and *not knowing* assumptions can be located within the educational philosophical work of Gert Biesta, and particularly *The Beautiful Risk of Education* (2015). In this text, he asserts the purpose of education as not only about filling a bucket, as a mere rational process, but rather about igniting a fire, with all the attendant risks that this presumes. Education as risk builds on earlier work in which he identifies three legitimate domains for educational practice, namely those associated with qualification, socialisation and subjectification (Biesta, 2009).

He takes qualification to mean, the gaining of 'Knowledge, skills and understanding that allow us to "do something"' (2009, p. 39) because this is one of the main purposes of education. Socialisation 'inserts individuals into existing ways of "doing" and "being"' (ibid., p. 40) and so allows children to be integrated into society and culture. However, subjectification, or 'ways of being that hint at independence from [existing] orders' (ibid., p. 40), is the aspect of practice that, in his view, is most overlooked and necessary for participation in a democracy, including the democratic spaces that young children occupy. Subjectification should therefore be 'fundamentally open and undetermined' (Biesta, 2011, p. 152) in ways that educate us to become citizens. Such ideas of open and undetermined democracy assume the possibility for transformative practices involving child and practitioner subjectivities in day-to-day practices (Rancière, 1991).

Subjectification relates to the principles of the *United Nations Convention on the Rights of the Child* (UNCRC, 1989) as laid out in *Birth to 5 Matters* (Early Years Coalition, 2021). The UNCRC claims the importance of children's voices as part of democracy where all voices can be listened to. This engages with the power of transformative practice and pedagogy to create spaces in which children can 'become more autonomous and independent in their thinking' (Biesta, 2011, p. 41).

Bronwyn Davies (2014) focuses on 'listening' to children in ways that require practitioners to be attentive subjects, so they might see and 'be' with children in new and creative ways. Her work links with the possibilities of Rancièrian transformation that afford something to come into being that wasn't there before. Listening is therefore 'emergent' for Davies (ibid., p. 21) in that it opens up:

> the possibility of coming to see life, and one's relation to it, in new and surprising ways. Emergent listening might begin with what is known, but it is open to creatively evolving into something new.

Davies draws inspiration from Reggio Emilia (Malaguzzi, 1993) practices, themselves a product of a post-war time when new democratic ways of human thriving were invoked by the community. Rinaldi (2006, p. 65), writing about Reggio Emilia, suggests these democratic practices evoke pedagogies that require 'suspension of judgements and above all prejudices'. Davies (2014, p. 13) describes the welcome of a 'Reggio-inspired ECEC community as that which does not allow anyone to assert a superior (or inferior) knowledge from outside', but rather to enter it as someone on an 'emergent project of discovery'.

In order to provide a supportive rather than instructional approach to working, practitioners at Green Shoots were each provided with a metaphorical 'toolbox'. This two-dimensional key visual contains clearly sign-posted elements that practitioners can consult when necessary, such as 'sustained shared thinking' (Siraj-Blatchford, 2009); Dynamic Risk Assessment (Pre-school Learning Alliance, 2017); the Three Pillars of Sustainability, highlighting inter-connections between the environment, economics and society; and 'reflection', which has long been central to quality ECEC practice.

What makes deployment of ECEC elements distinctive at Green Shoots is the 'diffractive' presumption of how they might to be utilised beyond the rational and instrumental. Diffraction is what happens when waves, washing up on a shoreline, come together, overlap and 'break apart in different directions' (Barad, 2007, p. 168). This helpful idea reminds practitioners that processes can be deployed in expectation of generating something new that wasn't there before.

Methodology

This case study focusses on relationships and processes (Denscombe, 2010) to investigate practice and pedagogy shaped by *not knowing* transformative ideals, with the role of the practitioner being the site of analysis. Research centres on semi-structured, conversational interviews, deliberately constructed to leave open space for deliberation and contingency, mirroring the nursery's transformative commitment. Interviews were conducted online by Rebecca and were individual, apart from the interview which involved the manager and deputy. Ten practitioners (out of twenty or so) volunteered to speak about their practitioner role. The sample, although small, was diverse, ranging in age from eighteen to mid-forties and with varied experience within ECEC between a few months to over twenty years.

Although it is usual to find different job titles within nursery settings, the only distinction between the practitioners interviewed was that of 'practitioner' and 'practitioner leader'. This commonality signifies core values and practices reflected in the data analysis below. All interviewees, including Kathy the co-author who was part of the interview sample, have been given pseudonyms to protect anonymity, including gender-neutral pronouns, as gender is not a variable explored in the data.

Further framing of this case requires researcher reflexivity ('self-questioning', Silverman, 2013, p. 125) to unpick aspects of power, ethics and knowledge claims. Kathy is known to Rebecca through academia and introduced Rebecca to the nursery as it underwent transformational changes that she was keen to document. Kathy acted as gatekeeper to negotiate research relationships as well as being a research participant. In order to bring a different 'gaze' and wider perspective to the analysis, Kathy did not have access to raw interview data, but instead acted as verifier of Rebecca's close readings of them. Kathy's role has been to critically query and question Rebecca, drawing on her own 'insider' subjectivity. Hence different positionalities, otherwise categorised as 'inside' and 'outside' (Chavez, 2008), bring an added layer of complexity to this case. We suggest such methodological complexity resonates with the power and potentiality of *not knowing* and the emergent subjectivities explored in the literature section. Indeed, Gallacher and Gallagher (2008) champion what they term as methodological 'ignorance' (ibid., p. 512); the enriching possibilities of qualitative research to hold open a space of research messiness, fostering new possibilities for what might be thought and known.

Data analysis

Dominant themes emerge from multiple readings of the data in which particular moments 'glow' (MacLure, 2013, p. 228). These have been abductively 'plugged in' (Jackson and Mazzei, 2012, p. 1) to readings of Rancièrian transformation and associated ideas of the purposes of education explored above, including subjectification and being open to change in ways that are uncertain. Each theme espouses an aspect of *not knowing* pedagogy and exposes interviewees' purposeful embrace of such practice as an entangled mixture of excitement, commitment, exhaustion and endless surprise.

'Our Community'

A Rancièrian idea of transformation as integrally connected to values emerges in what Robyn, the manager, has to say about changes over the last eighteen months:

> [This] process of transformation was not planned – I knew what my values were, but I didn't know how important it was to find people with similar values.

In recognising 'values', this addresses the challenges of opening up spaces of possibility where Robyn and the practitioners need to *'have difficult and uncomfortable conversations'*. This element of the Green Shoots is picked up by several of the practitioners; Max and Leslie express it slightly differently. Max explains the complexity of transformation and what it required of them, saying: *'We've asked for some big changes – I've struggled with it and I've hit brick walls and have had to go away and get my head around things'*. Leslie expresses some surprise that they *'feel comfortable to disagree, to make mistakes'* comparing this present role to previous workplaces where they have not felt confident to do so. Similarly, Rene notes, *'we are allowed to express our thoughts and feelings … it's okay to speak up'*.

The idea of a transformative community as one where voices can be heard, and listened to, in ways that accord with 'emergence' featured in many interviews. Adrian says:

> My views are taken seriously. … We are a team. Everyone's voice is important. What's the point of not saying if I am unhappy? Sometimes I just say it and I am surprised by what happens….

Adrian adds: *'I come from [names country] and I like to think that I bring different cultural perspectives'*. Adrian recognises that part of speaking out and being listened to is knowing that what one said might be challenging, but that the Nursery community is configured to cope with hearing difficult things. Although there are different practitioner roles with a range of responsibilities, Chris describes the community as espousing the ideals of a 'flattened hierarchy', where we have *'a sense of everyone's voice being valued and where we notice the different things that we each bring'*. Making no distinction between children and adults, they added *'it has to come from a place of respect and listening. This has to be embedded through everything'*.

Attention to a valuing that forms all relational possibilities, like the Reggio Emilia approach (Malaguzzi, 1993), was discussed by many interviewees. Chris explained working in family units with *'babies, toddlers and pre-schoolers'* all in one group or *'pod'* with key practitioners the children identify with, emphasising their attention to professional love:

> it really does feel more like a family … the older ones scaffold the learning of the younger children and they take on a role of responsibility and have a part to play … It is very beautiful to see.

Chris recognises that the benefits of family grouping was not immediate to everyone, and that for some, the adaptations took longer and were more painful. However, *'for others it was like a magic switch – especially apprentice practitioners who came out of themselves and became amazing role models'*. Bobby looks back and says that they now feel, *'really bad for the children [as things were before]'* because the new structure of the groupings *'gives them confidence and security'*. Charlie, who was *'sceptical at first'*, says *'I love it now'* because:

> It's so lovely to see big children looking after younger ones and a range of children playing together ... they [the younger children] have the chance to see and observe the big ones who are so caring as well. It's such a nice dynamic.

Max, not a *'huge fan'* of the idea of family groups initially, now feels it has *'broadened friendships [and made children] more independent, co-operative ... and the babies are having to figure things out themselves'*. Pat acknowledges, however, that this way of being in a community and showing respectful, engaged attention to the children means that: *'You do have to think on your feet all day as well as giving professional love [which] is emotionally draining.'* Alex feels the new system *'works'* because it requires a *'leap of faith'* that is built on *'trust'*, adding:

> I put a lot of faith in the judgement of my peers and the people I work with. X gives me good advice and I listen and then I think ... I ask lots of questions ... it's nice when we ask each other questions.

'Not Knowing'

So, how does Green Shoots translate into a *not knowing* space of practice where the process of being surprised, challenged or thinking differently can come about? The owner is quite blunt: *'People just agreeing with you all the time is just annoying.... I want to know that I am possibly not right, and this is about moving things. ...'* Adrian translates this permission into wider recognition of being prepared to be affected and changed for survival in the complex world of the twenty-first century, because *'things are constantly changing. The world is changing....my practice is changing.... I still don't know and that is okay. It has to be okay'*.

Chris captures the complexities of *not knowing*, reflecting on their responsibilities for colleagues new to the setting: *'It was a time of complete not-knowing for me, whilst also knowing the importance of giving the impression that I did!'*. They explain how coming back to Green Shoots after the refurbishment, there was a need *'to be much more in control of knowing about not knowing'*, reflecting through laughter their sense of the paradox of this. It meant being in a space of *'advocating for children but having to advocate also for everyone'*, *'letting go'* of stepping in, whilst maintaining a *'mask'* that *'everything is fine'*. They reflectively paused in their interview before describing the complex choreography of both *'knowing what's going on'* but also performing the role of *not knowing*. For all its huge demands, Chris recognises that *'transformation is now a daily thing'* but that in some nurseries *not knowing* might be *'squashed down because it is a hassle and more work to engage in reflective rather than routine action'*.

Frankie describes *not knowing* as being *'open-minded'* and *'whole-hearted'*, where *'it's okay not to know in order to be learning new ways and new things'*. Reflective time is now built into the fabric of the day, so that instead of writing individual reflective notes it has evolved into writing on a communal board of reflections that build throughout the day. This includes an imperative to practice the noticing of each child and their own *'unique wow moments'*. Frankie admits to sometimes thinking, *'Oh, what do I do!'* but picks up on the paradox that Chris asserted about *'being confident even as you are working things out'*. The community ethos helps this:

> You have other people around, and you can watch other people, and then you can try things next time ... it's good to have a positive and not a paranoid relationship with colleagues ... so you notice when it is about your own insecurities.

Frankie feels opportunities for open, reflective conversations with colleagues *'after a situation has happened'*, mean they never feel *'on their own'* when working things out.

'Stepping Back (and Stepping Up)'

Many practitioners were keen to describe aspects of their pedagogy and practice that chimed with transformative processes, capturing the moment-by-moment demands of their role. Charlie discussed a *not knowing* approach as one that enables children to realise that they *'don't have to be controlled by someone else ... that their opinions and their feelings matter'*. Practitioner sensibility is described as *'holding back'* to give *'children time to wonder'*, sometimes sitting and talking things through with colleagues, working out when it might be appropriate to make suggestions.

Frankie characterises their approach as only constructing activities for the children as *'an offer'* because *'the child might be in concentrated deep flow thinking or working on something else'*. Charlie is constantly surprised by the impact of this as they intraact together:

> It's so good to go with the flow and [the children] really help you build on your skills and stuff because you are helping them....I have found out so many things because they want to investigate....what's bigger: a T Rex or a whale?.... we researched it in all sorts of ways and then we discussed it and made all sorts of models out of clay. I asked the children, 'how do you think we find this out?' The children suggested a book and then the computer. It's a whole new learning curve...I am learning again about how to hold-back and not take over.

Alex uses musical metaphors to characterise aspects of the practitioner role, asserting it is not about assumptions of *'adult-led activities'* but focused on finding out what the children are interested in. It is *'not making the children dance to our tune but rather about finding out the tune of the children and playing the harp along with them in harmony'*. For Max, practice is less about *'getting the jobs done – screw that – it's about listen, observe, wait … I feel closer to [the children] for it and celebrate their achievements and feel their pain more'*. Max's acknowledgement of *not knowing* encompasses a whole gamut of behaviours, sensibilities, dispositions, excitements and frustrations, including more difficult feelings.

Equally, Chris describes the practitioner role as complex, being an attentive, uncertain guide who *'is listening to everything [the children] are communicating – including with their bodies as well'*. Leslie proposes that this means *'bringing the children into every part of the planning that goes on'*. This is hugely demanding and requires belief in a community to work things out together:

> So, our role is to hear that voice [of the child] first and to think what we can add to that to make them curious…. I have to extend that voice somehow without taking over … without thinking about what they ought to achieve….

'Becoming affected: feeling, doing, and being vulnerable'

Several practitioners described ways they are affected by daily encounters. There were many expressions, of *'joy'*; *'excitement'*; *'complete engagement in what I'm doing'*; *'curiosity'*; as well as finding it *'hugely challenging'* to be in a space where *'it's okay not to know and to find things out'*. One leader recalled that changing from one way of doing things was *'very difficult for some people – unlearning is very hard – the whole world is upside down – same building, same children but a complete shift'*.

Chris reflects on *not knowing* as engaging a range of intellectual and emotional dispositions for reflection. Indeed, the nursery *'toolbox'* contains the image of a torch to remind practitioners to shine a light back on themselves to check how they are thinking and feeling. Such an opportunity gives permission *'to be vulnerable and open to making mistakes'*. Chris admits that this had sometimes been a struggle: *'In my head I was advocating for this all along but in practice I was often very certain and in control'*.

Bobby considers that encouragement to engage affectively means that, *'even on down- days you have to force yourself to connect with the children'* and that *'you can cope'*. This approach means *'you are constantly alert to the children's moods and feelings'* and *'how to react to them'*. Bobby shares ways to talk about their own feelings with the children who *'can be very empathetic and interested'*, surprising Bobby initially. Similarly, Alex discusses negotiating ways of *'making mistakes'* such that other practitioners and children can see this as a part of the emotional journey of enjoying *'finding out and learning'*.

'Engaging the human and the more-than-human'.

For Robyn, the manager, and Billie, the deputy, finding a way to connect transformative pedagogies of feelings and relationships with caring for the wider world, including animals and plants, is a crucial dimension of change at Green Shoots. Childcare *'was so wasteful [of material resources]'*, explains Robyn. In redesigning outdoor and indoor spaces to create one free-flowing environment, Billie highlights that they were faced with the challenge of, *'what are the children going to play with [outside]?'* However, by remaining committed to the ideals of Reggio Emilia (Malaguzzi, 1993) they held onto their belief in *'focusing on unlocking something special and challenging for a generation of young people'*.

As the forest garden became established, Robyn and Billie can see that being in the garden is *'the children's education ... we realised that they were all learning'*. Rene is delighted with the ongoing opportunities afforded by children's intimate relationships with plants, organic materials and small creatures that they find together and care for in the garden. *'It's not like any other nursery ... it's so sustainable, so eco-friendly and so free-flow ... every minute and every day is different!'* Frankie embraces the fact that nothing is *'set in stone for how things might happen'* enjoying the *'open space where children can have their freedom and go anywhere'*. They talk about children *'touching the soil, or the grass and having the connection with raw materials: it's just great'*. They can *'find a worm, gently hold it and be really fascinated. We are all learning so much'*. Pat discusses making dinosaurs out of sticks and pinecones which *'leads to us making many more games'*. The children are *'just really curious about things'*.

'Diffractively deploying the toolbox'

The toolbox was created to support practitioners with uneasy feeling of loss as they shifted from predominantly adult-led activities to a transformative journey approach. Chris says *'What many practitioners struggled with was "not getting involved"'*. Practitioners have gradually learnt about each of the toolbox approaches and come to consider situations where they might bring one of them into play. Max recalls that practitioners were initially given reflective time together to engage with the toolbox, to consider issues *'such as the Characteristics of effective learning, Leuven scales, and child-initiated learning ... that's when things really started to change'*. Chris felt this gave practitioners something *'concrete'* to reflect on. They could ask, *'is this the right tool for this time?'* Chris explains that reflecting on when, where, why and how tools might be used *'depends on an intra-action in a space of not knowing. That's the point. We are not constantly quizzing the child asking, 'what are you doing? Rather we are observing, waiting and listening and learning with the child'*.

Alex likens using the toolbox to being a good cook: *'You have to be able to think and do many things at one time and you certainly draw on your experience – you get to know that the salt in the onion will be better put in at one particular moment in a process rather than another'*. Knowing they can draw on the toolbox whilst patiently observing, waiting and listening means that Alex has *'learnt not to be authoritative – it doesn't work* and then I have seen children copying my approach [being authoritative] which is not good'. Frankie considers that '*observing, waiting, listening*', could suggest to an outsider that, '*we might be sitting back, but we are constantly looking out for when to interject*'. Adrian recognises this approach as very different to how they performed in the past:

> when I started I jumped in on everything. I've learnt to sit back and only jump in if absolutely necessary – it's taught me patience. Children can sort their own problems. Seeing how arguments get sorted between the children – they can do it … shows their capabilities and their ingenuity as humans. But I used to be so different!

Frankie comments that the dynamic risk-assessment tool helps ensure children are involved in decision-making in ways that engage them '*emotionally*'. They reflect that, '*life is full of risks … so the sooner they learn this the better*'. Using this approach '*exemplifies how capable children are … they learn to teach other, which I think is more powerful than an adult saying something*'. Frankie draws on relating children's feelings to a range of different colours, as a supportive way of encouraging them to '*feel okay about the fact that life is emotional*'.

Bobby notices the children often go off and '*find things themselves*', spending '*lots of time with things they assemble*'. They feel that '*the children's' concentration is better [than when designed around adult-orchestrated activities] because it is about their own loves … working with loose parts means the possibilities for play are endless*'. Alex feels the children spend a lot of time in imaginary worlds in '*role play – arguments – lots of things happen*' and reflects that their job '*is to seed and to plant possibilities whether with marbles, scarves, sand, leaves, twigs, any stuff that they can use*'. This role is '*subtle … I have to decide when or whether to intervene, recognising the wheels turning … sometimes you do have to give a gentle nudge, drawing on the toolbox*'.

Conclusion

This chapter has explored a journey of transformative practice and pedagogy in one nursery. It has demonstrated how it is possible to champion ways for practitioners and children to work democratically, finding a voice and embracing *not knowing* together. The case study has connected with practitioners, the manager and deputy through dialogic interviews, engaging those involved in reflecting on their shifting roles. Practitioners detailed how ideas of community have been reworked and reasserted as relational. This intimately connects to difficulty, and difference of feelings and perspective as productive, in ways that chime with a hopeful Rancièrian logic of transformation occurring moment-by-moment. Practitioners discussed the intricate, creative choreographies of their subtle practice-pedagogic roles. These require them to be with, and to pay attention to, children and colleagues in the rich, intra-active possibilities of their sustainable, free-flow environment. This is challenging work. It requires self-critique and reflection, alongside an assumption of Rancièrian equality (1991) where all practitioners have knowledge and experiences that warrant them being taken seriously. Chris captures the ethical commitment to working together with contingency and curiosity in this remark to a practitioner seeking a definitive response about how to act: *'I don't know, isn't it exciting? But let's work this out together!'*.

The transformative approach at Green Shoots re-envisions the subjectivities of practitioner and child alike in asserting the possibilities for democratic knowing, doing and being, recognizing this as part of the history of the demanding role of the ECP. It suggests that, given time, space and will, it is always possible to shift between routine and reflexive actions (Dewey, 1933) that can inform, and be informed by, being open to *not knowing*.

REFLECTIVE POINTS

1. Consider how your setting reflects ideas of democracy as suggested in this chapter. Are there opportunities for practitioners and children to be listened to and taken seriously, even in moments of disagreement?
2. What opportunities are there for reflection and *not knowing* in your setting? Think about this especially in relation to working with others, in ways that assume the possibility of being changed by the experience

---

References

Barad, K. (2007). *Meeting the universe halfway: Quantum physics and the entanglement of matter and meaning*. Durham and London: Duke University Press.

Biesta, G.L. (2009). Good education in an age of measurement: On the need to reconnect with the question of purpose in education. *Educational assessment Evaluation and Accountability* (formerly: Journal of Personnel Evaluation in Education), 21(1), 33–46.

Biesta, G.L. (2011). *Learning democracy in school and society*. Rotterdam: Sense Publishers.

Biesta, G.L. (2015). *The Beautiful risk of education*. London: Routledge.

Biesta, G.L. Bingham, C. and Rancière, J. (2010*). Jacques Rancière : Education, truth, emancipation*. London: Continuum International Publishing Group.

Chavez, C. (2008). Conceptualizing from the inside: Advantages, complications, and demands on the insider positionality. *The Qualitative Report*, 13(3), 474–494.

Davies, B. (2014). *Listening to children: Being and becoming*. New York: Routledge.

Denscombe, M. (2010). *The good research guide: For small-scale social research projects*. Maidenhead, Berkshire: McGraw-Hill.

Department for Education (2020). *Development matters: Non- statutory curriculum guidance for the early years foundation stage*. London: Crown.

Department for Education (2021). *Statutory framework for the early years foundation stage. Setting the standards for learning, development and care for children from birth to five*. London: Crown.

Dewey, J. (1933). *How we think: A restatement of the relation of reflective thinking to the educative process*. Chicago, IL: Henry Regnery and Co.

Dunne, É. and Seery, A. (2016). *The pedagogics of unlearning*. Santa Barbara, CA: Punctum books.
Early Years Coalition (2021). *Birth to five matters*. St. Albans: Early Education.
Gallacher, L.A. and Gallagher, M. (2008). Methodological immaturity in childhood research? Thinking through participatory methods. *Childhood*, 15(4), 499–516.
Jackson, A.Y. and Mazzei, L.A. (2012). *Thinking with theory in qualitative research, viewing data across multiple perspectives*. London and New York: Routledge.
Jones, K. (2013). The right and the left. *Changing English*, 20(4), 328–340.
MacLure, M. (2013). The wonder of data. *Critical Methodologies*, 13(4), 228–232.
Malaguzzi, L. (1993). No Way. The Hundred is There (L.Gandini translation), in C. Edwards, L. Gandini and G. Foreman (Eds.), *The hundred languages of children; The Reggio Emilia experience in transformation* (1st edition, p. 3) Ablex, NJ: Norwood.
Murris, K. (2016). *The posthuman child: Educational transformation through philosophy with picturebooks*. London: Routledge.
Gibson, J.L., Cornell, M. & Gill, T. (2017). A Systematic Review of Research into the Impact of Loose Parts Play on Children's Cognitive, Social and Emotional Development. *School Mental Health* 9, 295–309.
Pre-school Learning Alliance. (2017). *Dynamic risk management in the early years*, England and Wales: Pre-school Learning Alliance.
Rancière, J. (1991). *The ignorant schoolmaster, five lessons in intellectual emancipation*, trans. Kristin Ross. Stanford, CA: Stanford University Press.
Rancière, J. (2004). Who is the subject of the rights of man? *The South Atlantic Quarterly*, 103(2/3), 297–310.
Rinaldi, C. (2006). *In dialogue with Reggio Emilia: Listening, researching and learning*. London, Routledge: Psychology Press.
Silverman, D. (2013). *Doing qualitative research: A practical handbook*. London and New York: Sage Publications.
Siraj-Blatchford, I. (2009). Conceptualising progression in the pedagogy of play and sustained shared thinking in early childhood education: A Vygotskian perspective. *Education and Child Psychology*, 26(2), 77–89.
UNCRC. (1989). *The United Nations convention on the rights of the child*. United Nations, https://www.unicef.org.uk/wp-content/uploads/2010/05/UNCRC_united_nations_convention_on_the_rights_of_the_child.pdf
UNESCO. (2017). *Education for Sustainable development goals: learning objectives*. Paris, France: United Nations Education, Scientific and Cultural Organization.
Webb, R. and Foster, K. (2020). The inspiring pedagogy and practice of ignorance: Reflections on the use of a particular scrapbook approach in the early years nursery to facilitate curiosity and engagement. *Foundation Stage Forum*, https://eyfs.info/articles.html/general/the-inspiring-pedagogy-and-practice-of-ignorance-reflections-on-the-use-of-a-particular-scrapbook-approach-in-the-early-years-nursery-to-facilitate-curiosity-and-engagement-r318/

10
RECONCEPTUALISING QUALITY INTERACTIONS

Hayley Preston-Smith

Introduction

This chapter explores and challenges views of 'quality' and 'quality interaction' in Early Childhood Education and Care (ECEC), foregrounding the Early Childhood Practitioner's (ECP's) perspectives and experiences. Exploring this concept is not novel, on the contrary, quality has been the subject of many publications over 30 years (for example, Siraj-Blatchford et al., 2002; Sylva et al., 2004; Dahlberg, Moss and Pence, 2007; Melhuish and Gardiner, 2018). Yet despite this, the concept of quality itself remains a contested term, with some implementing objectivity and measurability for an outcomes-based position, and others focusing upon quality as a process. Similar debates permeate discussions of quality interactions within ECEC. In this chapter I assert that quality interactions require recognition of both child and ECP subjectivity emerging in the process of social communication and relationship building as cornerstones of practice.

The concept of quality, and quality interaction between practitioner and child, is often assumed as a means to an end, rather than a 'values good' in its own right (Rudoe, 2020). Documentation such as *Development Matters* (Early Education, 2012) and Ofsted's *Early Years Inspection Handbook* (2019) encourage regular ECP-child interactions to promote good developmental outcomes, and to provide outstanding practice. By encouraging ECPs to take on prescribed views of quality interaction, there is a danger of this becoming yet another way of children meeting instrumental policy objectives, rather than addressing the needs of the unique child as a social actor.

As highlighted throughout this book, there are serious issues with the conceptualisation of the ECP within policy discourse, often presenting the practitioner as little more than someone who can 'prove' that they meet the statutory requirements of the sector. Additionally, there is considerable critique concerning the lack of attention to ECP voice and values within curriculum and policy frameworks, with those working within ECEC often marginalised from decision-making within the sector (Powell, 2010; Brock, 2012; Basford, 2019). Consequently, the aim of this chapter is to challenge reductionist and restrictive views of quality interaction, and to begin highlighting practitioner-informed approaches with the voice and values of the ECP at the forefront.

(Re)Defining quality interactions in ECEC

There are many perspectives of quality interactions, as, in common with so much of ECEC, the concept is hard to pin-down. Interest around quality interaction with young children primarily emerged from Researching Effective Pedagogy in the Early Years (REPEY, Siraj-Blatchford et al., 2002) and Effective Provision of Pre-School Education (EPPE, Sylva et al., 2004) projects, both of which emphasised the direct link between high-quality learning environments and children's future progress. It was through these projects that the impact of quality interaction between ECPs and children was highlighted and Sustained Shared Thinking (SST)[1] promoted as 'a necessary prerequisite for excellent early years practice', due to its impact on children's cognitive achievement (Sylva et al., 2004, p. 36). SST became an essential component of quality interaction, leading the way to a concept of quality, which can be measured as 'outcomes' for children, with variables such as qualification levels influencing the level of quality outcomes and outputs of the setting.

Principles highlighted by the reports above have had significant influence on ensuing ECEC documentation. Unsurprisingly these documents align quality interactions to children's outcomes, with the *Inspection Handbook* encouraging inspectors to observe how ECPs utilise interactions to encourage independence, expression of thought, inclusion of 'new words', hypothesising and testing new ideas, and solving problems (Ofsted, 2019, p. 16). Whilst not specifically stating that ECPs *must* provide quality interactions within their practice, the previous *Early Years Foundation Stage* (EYFS) encouraged regular 'warm' and 'positive' interactions, with a view to guiding children through developmental targets (DfE, 2017). The revised EYFS (DfE, 2021) and *Development Matters* guidance (DfE, 2020) promote a stronger focus on interactions whereby ECPs can create opportunities for children to be exposed to 'new vocabulary' within conversations (DfE, 2020, p. 8).

Such policy documents have created a discourse of quality that is situated within measurability and school readiness, which ultimately places an expectation on children who are 'unready' to be pushed towards the 'ready child' status (Evans, 2015, p. 32). Essentially, the discourse surrounding quality interactions in contemporary ECEC is judged by 'specific measures of child outcomes at developmental stages' (Rudoe, 2020, p. 1016). This not only places pressure on the child but also promotes a view that ECPs need to carefully design interactions to push children towards predetermined outcomes, which can result in forced and unnatural communication (Fisher, 2016).

Any universal definition of quality, and in turn quality interactions, remains elusive, with Elfer, Goldschmied and Selleck (2012, p. 3) presenting it as a 'slippery idea'. Dahlberg, Moss and Pence (2007) attribute this ambiguity to the subjective nature of quality itself, a concept wholly dependent on one's perspective of the world that is often taken-for-granted. The notion that quality can be narrowed to a universal meaning fails to account for the significance of context. Moss (2016, p. 9) states that quality 'could have so many meanings as to become effectively meaningless in discourse and useless as a tool of evaluation'.

The recently published *Birth to 5 Matters* (Early Years Coalition, EYC, 2021) guidance, an alternative to the revised *Development Matters* document, provides a section outlining the role of interactions within ECEC from an ECP perspective. A key point is that adults should only support children when needed. Crucially, the ECP is expected to step 'back' in order to prevent interrupting children's play and thinking (EYC, 2021, p. 19), suggesting that, paradoxically, quality interactions can sometimes be about less immediate interaction and interruption, and rather more about watching, waiting and listening.

Research methodology

This small-scale research project took place in a Reception class of a primary school in the South East of England, and comprised semi-structured interviews with one class teacher and a teaching assistant, along with observations of ECP-child interactions taking place over a period of one month. The overall aim was to gauge insight into participants' perspectives of quality interaction with children in their classroom and how they arrived at these viewpoints. I had completed my Early Years Teacher Status (EYTS) training at this school and the participants were happy to support me in carrying out research. Knowing them well meant that they could 'open up' and discuss their ideas and experiences without fear of judgement (O'Reilly, Ronzoni and Dogra, 2013).

Taking an unstructured approach (McKechnie, 2008), observations were video recorded using the classroom iPad, not only to capture specificities of speech but also body language and detail of the activity being undertaken. Following the observations, I interviewed the class teacher and teaching assistant to gain their perspectives on the nature of the interaction between them and the child. These interviews took a semi-structured approach (Brinkmann and Kvale, 2018), to allow room to explore avenues I had not foreseen.

It is important to note that, due to the small sample size, this data was never intended to be generalisable. What this very small-scale project did succeed in doing was to provoke thought and open discussions concerning the possibilities of reconceptualising quality interaction within ECEC and the role of the ECP in determining what might be said about it.

Reanimating the data

Thematic analysis enabled continuous reflection on data to account for new political and social contexts, recognising that nothing is ever completely set in stone (Wästerfors, Åkerström and Jacobsson, 2013). It is clear that the context of ECEC constantly changes, leading me to seek further nuance within my previous findings and explore concepts that may not have been within the scope of the previous analytic method (Roulston, 2001). For this second round of analysis, I used Interpretative Phenomenological Analysis (IPA), adopting a careful balance between the meanings of the ECPs' and my own perspectives (Smith, Flowers and Larkin, 2009; Peoples, 2021). In its re-animation and re-analysis, the data has taken on new meanings, highlighting some relevant debates within current discussions and everyday ECEC contexts.

Revisiting the original findings

Original analysis of the data found that the interviews provided insight into the ECPs' perspectives of a quality interaction with children, from which key themes emerged. The observations allowed me to experience these interactions as they occurred and highlighted ideas that were not necessarily discussed during the interviews, but that nonetheless appeared to support the ECPs' views. The main themes that emerged from exploring the ECPs' conceptualisations and experiences of a quality interaction with children included: questioning (both open-ended and structured), encouragement (through praise and questioning), praise (verbal and through body language) and understanding (through questioning and observing the children).

Whilst this analytic process provided some suggestions as to how each ECP perceived quality interaction, it also left open opportunities for further examination, especially where contradictions arose in the practitioners' statements. Consider these examples:

> ...what the result is would then, I suppose, decide on whether [the interaction] was quality or not.
>
> *(Kimberly, class teacher)*

> You've got to have happy children who are happy to talk to each other.
>
> *(Daisy, teaching assistant)*

Although both ECPs discussed similar ideas that they felt created a quality interaction, such as extending learning, and social-emotional aspects of subjectivity, Daisy's overall conceptualisation of quality interaction depended on ascertaining a child's everyday emotional well-being. On the other hand, Kimberly stated that developmental outcomes must, ultimately, determine the quality of each child-practitioner interaction. This meant that quality could only be measured with hindsight, and would be measured against an outcomes instrument. These contrasting responses led me to conclude that, although both participants worked within the same environment, their ECP identity and role within the classroom determined their individual scope to conceptualise quality interaction. As the class teacher, Kimberly primarily worked within a whole-class situation, and focused on leading children towards developmental goals and indicators that she must meet in order to be a 'successful' class teacher. As the teaching assistant, Daisy was responsible for more small-group or individual interactions where she had latitude to focus on social interaction and well-being.

Other factors that influenced initial analysis of the data from both participants were linked to their qualifications and the specificities of their teaching experience. Kimberly had been teaching within the reception class for two years, and primarily within Key Stage 1 during her Qualified Teacher Status (QTS) training. Daisy had worked in early years settings for five years and had obtained Early Years Teacher Status (EYTS) 2 years previously. It was clear from Kimberly's observations and her interview that the interactions she provided were more focused on children's measurable outcomes, as she often referred to their 'results', 'language' and 'knowledge'. Kimberly viewed her role in the classroom as a guide to a specific end for the children, saying:

> If there's a child you're targeting, for example, speech or social and emotional, then you would actually take time out and sit with them.

Daisy's role, in comparison, was that of a co-constructor; someone to support children both academically and emotionally, and able to follow their interests which might take-off in a new direction from that originally intended:

> I suppose it's listening to the child, understanding what they are saying to you, communicating … feeding back to you, acting on what they're saying … using what they are doing to push them further….

New insights: The multifaceted role of the ECP in the quality interaction

Although the original analysis noted how each participant reflected on their particular remit and role, this new analysis revealed ways that they shifted between a range of different subjective identities during the time I was with them. Whereas the previous analysis used observations to support interview data, the IPA analytical method allowed for a more comprehensive analysis of each observation transcript. In re-engaging with the data, I was able to ascertain that there were occasions when both practitioners recognised that the ECP undertakes significant 'costume changes' in terms of their role and relationships, depending on the context and specific needs of children in the moment. These shaped the quality of the interaction. Within one interview, for example, Kimberly discussed a 'leader' identity in which there is an adult to guide children through activities towards an end-goal, whereby the child arrives at the 'correct answer'.

Similarly, within one of Kimberly's observations, whilst working with the whole class during a maths session involving the two times table, a child struggled with what came after 10, often answering with 11. Kimberly reminded the child of the 'miss one, say one' rule when counting in twos; she became 'leader', guiding the child through to the correct answer. Daisy also displays a 'leader' identity when helping a child who was struggling with a kangaroo fact-writing activity. By prompting the child with questions, such as 'what else did you learn about kangaroos?', she was able to lead the child through the activity.

Within Daisy's interview, however, despite displaying examples of leading children through tasks, she did not discuss a 'leader' identity as an attribute of her ECP subjectivity. Instead, Daisy viewed her role as supporting children's learning. She elaborated by highlighting the importance of a holistic approach with the children she encountered:

> [I] scaffold what they're learning, what they're doing and help them with interactions with other children and adults so it's like a whole rounded approach, it's not just … it's not just the talking *at* them.

Likewise, despite a key aspect of her role being to lead children towards preset targets, Kimberly also discussed the pastoral side of the practitioner role, as a support network for the children, both emotionally and academically:

> the children would actually … are happy to talk to [adults] in any situation, whether they've been hurt or whether they're just seeking help… in lesson time … or just in general so they're comfortable to talk to [adults].

For example, within the maths observation mentioned above, it was clear that the child was feeling unhappy, which prompted Kimberly to step in and offer support. Therefore, what was originally interpreted as leading to a target could also be viewed as providing emotional support.

When discussing how quality interactions were implemented, Daisy did not specify a particular technique. She explained the need for flexibility, stressing that the direction of the interaction must change according to the context:

> Some of it you have to think on your feet and … change it … it also depends on what the children are doing … because that might then change … take you off on a totally different direction.

Despite my initial reading of divergent views of the two ECPs, I came to re-read the data in such a way as to see that they both demonstrated many different roles within their interactions with the children. Upon re-examination I could see that both believed their roles constituted many different identities, not just 'class teacher who instructs' and 'teaching assistant who supports and guides'. These roles included being a friend, a source of reassurance, a co-constructor, someone who articulates open questions, and who aims to be a good role model, promoting positive body language and speech within the classroom. For the first time, I noticed how their identities changed in response to the interests or needs of the children within specific interactions, and that this might then reshape the direction that the interaction took.

Pressures of performativity and accountability

Another theme that I noticed upon re-analysis was the pressure of accountability. This was highlighted primarily within Kimberley's data. Throughout her interview, she linked the quality of her interactions to the child's academic and developmental outcomes. She also discussed using interactions as a tool for 'targeting' children who may be identified as 'lower level' and using observations as a tool for evidencing developmental outcomes. She said:

> I think that makes the difference and setting things up … there's a lot they learned from it and we … well I got loads of observations.

Kimberly expressed concerns about not collecting enough evidence of children's progress and used interactions that she 'set up' in order to rectify this, usually within child-initiated time.[2] These interactions were ultimately undertaken in the context of expectations of meeting external accountability criteria. Many of Kimberly's responses highlighted the issue with trying to work around her responsibilities as class teacher, much like trying to balance several spinning plates at one time.

This accountability pressure was not reflected in Daisy's interview responses, as she primarily discussed the need to follow the children's lead and allow for flexibility within interactions, due to their spontaneity. She said:

> If you've got a timetable which is really rigid, and there's no chance for deviating away from that, there's gonna … restrict what you can do with the children.

Kimberly's responses reflected her role as responsible for the measurable outcomes of the children (Roberts-Holmes, 2020). Kimberly also discusses techniques used by other teachers that she knows, comparing her own practice to theirs:

> … so you're saying about evaluating things, in their choosing time, in theory it's meant to be like a Plan, Do, Review type thing, and I know loads of schools do Plan, Do, Review …

This provides an insight into the pressures that ECPs, like Kimberly, face when engaging in quality interactions against a backdrop of competing demands. It also provides a rationale for the divergence between some of the views of the class teacher and the teaching assistant.

Discussion

My original project aimed to provide a representation of what ECPs perceive as the primary components of quality interactions. However, taking a more phenomenological approach to analysis of the data allowed for a deeper understanding of the ECPs' 'lived experiences' of interaction, and highlighted important issues that they face in everyday practice. One notable feature was the multifaceted nature of their subjectivities that change and shape the interaction contextually, despite the constraints of the accountable classroom teacher. Participants' interview responses emphasised their specific roles within quality interaction, yet my observational data acknowledged how different identities were dependent on the child's interests and needs, moving away from the prescription of 'class teacher' and 'teaching assistant' identities.

Within their interviews, both ECPs identified their role as a support mechanism for children, to provide assistance or reassurance when needed. But they also viewed the child as capable within their own learning; similar to Malaguzzi (1993) and Moss (2016) who both view the child as an active learner requiring sensitive encouragement and support. Daisy was often observed adapting her practice to follow the child's lead. Whilst Kimberly also discussed the need to let children be active within their own learning, she had to balance this with her other class teacher responsibilities, such as planning, assessing children's progress, and accounting for her decisions. Kimberly is not alone as she is 'caught' in the conundrum of a complex and demanding role as a class teacher, where she is often 'left too busy and preoccupied with meeting standards to wrestle with their professional identit[y]' (Osgood, 2006, p. 6).

The ECP role is a conflicting and conflicted one, as revealed in the re-animation and re-analysis of my data. It is one where many, like Kimberly, find themselves torn between their pedagogical values, academic pressures and the drive for 'standards'; 'trying to be all things to all people' (Basford, 2019, p. 799). Demands created by contemporary policies, such as those published by Ofsted (2019), have created a system whereby quality is considered achievable through 'constructs of regulation, accountability, measurability, excellent/best practice, standardisation', and as a result space for autonomy and more alternative views is reduced (Osgood, 2006, p. 739). ECPs are constricted by the 'datafication' of ECEC (Roberts-Holmes and Bradbury, 2016), and a neoliberal system which holds them accountable for the 'successes' or 'failures' of the children within their care (Roberts-Holmes, 2020) bringing with it a pressing need to evidence that children have reached particular developmental or academic milestones. The consequence of these additional pressures on the ECP is less time to 'be' in the moment of the interaction, and a risk of providing interactions that resemble 'chocolate-dipped-broccoli' (Bruckman, 1999, p. 75); in other words, the agendas of assessment and outcomes are disguised as more palatable, but often trite, interactional conversations.

The divergence of some of the responses to questions about quality interaction would seem to be due to differing roles and responsibilities. Both Barkham (2008) and Butt and Lowe (2012) describe the class teacher as chiefly responsible for the outcomes of the class as a whole, whilst the teaching assistant is most often required to take on more of a supporting role, working with individual children in a way that can cope with contingency and unpredictability. This may explain why Kimberley primarily discussed 'leading', whilst Daisy referred to her role as 'support', despite my observation of them shifting in and out of leading and supporting roles.

Reconceptualising quality interactions – Where do we go from here?

The consequence of this re-analysis is the painting of a more nuanced picture of ECPs as ever-changing and adaptive in their identity and subjectivity; and who feel the constraints of the discourses that shape their quality interactions (whether these emanate from existing policy, performativity, or accountability pressures). Both examinations of data suggest that there are multitudinous perspectives of a quality interaction, even for those with defined 'fixed' practitioner roles within the same environment.

The concept of quality interaction needs to be reconceptualised as more fluid, dynamic and context-contingent if ECPs are to bring their knowledge about the children and context to light. As we know, the concept of quality within quality interactions, and within ECEC as a whole, is problematic and narrow. Dahlberg, Moss and Pence (2007) suggest that there are many 'languages of evaluation' that should be considered, calling for further research to explore the experiences and conceptualisations of a quality interaction, including from the child's perspective, as well as the ECP.

At the present time, there seems to be a shift towards a more practitioner-led decision-making process through publication of the *Birth to 5 Matters* (Early Years Coalition, 2021), but we are still a long way away from the autonomous ECP with reflexive space to justify the decisions they make in relation to quality and engaging quality interactions. Perspectives on the nature of quality within ECEC have been limited (Rudoe, 2020), so for authentic change to take place, we need a shift towards a greater representation of the knowledgeable ECP voice within policy documents. This would give EC practitioners an opportunity to 'rethink what matters most in education' (Azorín, 2020, p. 381) and to question if current guidelines around quality interaction bear any resemblance to what they think should be prioritised in their own future practice.

> **REFLECTIVE POINTS**
>
> Reflect on quality interactions in relation to your practice in ECEC.
>
> 1. What does a quality interaction in ECEC look like and feel like to you?
> 2. How has this been shaped by your own experiences in practice?
> 3. How might you be reflexive with your practitioner colleagues about the quality interaction as a process?

Notes

1 Siraj-Blatchford et al define this concept as *'an episode in which two or more individuals "work together" in an intellectual way to solve a problem, clarify a concept, evaluate activities, extend a narrative, etc. Both parties must contribute to the thinking and it must develop and extend'* (2002, p. 8). See Siraj-Blatchford et al. (2002) and Sylva et al. (2004) for more detail.
2 Child-initiated time (or child-initiated play/learning) is defined by *Birth to 5 Matters* as a period of time whereby *'a child determines the activity – what they will use, what they will do, who is involved'* (Early Years Coalition, 2021, p. 118).

References

Azorín, C. (2020) 'Beyond COVID-19 Supernova: Is Another Education Coming?', *Journal of Professional Capital and Community*, 5(3/4), pp. 381–390.

Barkham, J. (2008) 'Suitable Work for Women? Roles, Relationships and Changing Identities of "Other Adults' in the Early Years Classroom"', *British Educational Research Journal*, 34(6), pp. 839–853.

Basford, J. (2019) 'The Early Years Foundation Stage: Whose Knowledge, Whose Values?', *Education 3-13*, 47(7), pp. 779–783.

Brinkmann, S. and Kvale, S. (2018) *Doing Interviews*, 2nd ed, London: SAGE Publications Ltd.

Brock, A. (2012) 'Building a Model of Early Years Professionalism from Practitioners' Perspectives', *Journal of Early Childhood Research*, 11(1), pp. 27–44.

Bruckman, A. (1999) 'Can Educational Be Fun?', *Game Developers Conference*, California, 17th March 1999, Atlanta: Georgia Institute of Technology, pp. 75–79.

Butt, R. and Lowe, K. (2012) 'Teaching Assistants and Class Teachers: Differing Perceptions, Role Confusion and the Benefits of Skills-Based Training', *International Journal of Inclusive Education*, 16(2), pp. 207–219.

Dahlberg, G., Moss, P. and Pence, A. (2007) *Beyond Quality in Early Childhood Education and Care: Languages of Evaluation*, 2nd edition, Oxon: Routledge.

Department for Education (DfE) (2017) *Statutory Framework for the Early Years Foundation Stage Setting the Standards for Learning, Development and Care for Children from Birth to Five*, available at: https://www.foundationyears.org.uk/files/2017/03/EYFS_STATUTORY_FRAMEWORK_2017.pdf (Accessed 27 July 2021).

Department for Education (DfE) (2020) *Development Matters: Non-Statutory Guidance for the Early Years Foundation Stage*, available at: https://assets.publishing.service.gov.uk/government/uploads/system/uploads/attachment_data/file/944603/Development_Matters_-_non-statuatory_cirriculum_guidance_for_EYFS.pdf (Accessed 9 June 2021).

Department for Education (DfE) (2021) *Statutory Framework for the Early Years Foundation Stage (EYFS)*, available at: https://assets.publishing.service.gov.uk/government/uploads/system/uploads/attachment_data/file/974907/EYFS_framework_-_March_2021.pdf (Accessed 27 July 2021).

Early Education (2012) *Development Matters in the Early Years Foundation Stage (EYFS)*, London: Early Education.

Early Years Coalition (EYC) (2021) *Birth to 5 Matters: Guidance by the Sector, For the Sector*, St Alban's: Early Education.

Elfer, P., Goldschmied, E. and Selleck, D.Y. (2012) *Key Persons in the Early Years*, 2nd edition, Oxon: Routledge.

Evans, K. (2015) 'Reconceptualizing Dominant Discourses in Early Childhood Education: Exploring Readiness as an Active-Ethical-Relation', *Complicity: An International Journal of Complexity and Education*, 12(1), pp. 32–51.

Fisher, J. (2016*) Interacting or Interfering? Improving Interactions in the Early Years*, Maidenhead: Open University Press.

Malaguzzi, L. (1993) 'For an Education Based on Relationships', *Young Children*, 49(1), pp. 9–13.

McKechnie, L.E.F. (2008) 'Unstructured Observation', in Given, L.M. (ed.), *The Sage Encyclopedia of Qualitative Research Methods*, London: SAGE Publications Ltd., pp. 907–908.

Melhuish, E. and Gardiner, J. (2018) *Study of Early Education and Development (SEED): Impact Study on Early Education Use and Child Outcomes up to Age Four Years*, London: DfE.

Moss, P. (2016) 'Why Can't We Get Beyond Quality?', *Contemporary Issues in Early Childhood*, 17(1), pp. 8–15.

Office for Standards in Education (Ofsted) (2019) *Early Years Inspection Handbook for Ofsted Registered Provision*, available at: https://assets.publishing.service.gov.uk/government/uploads/system/uploads/attachment_data/file/828465/Early_years_inspection_handbook.pdf (Accessed 26 March 2020).

O'Reilly, M., Ronzoni, P. and Dogra, N. (2013) *Research with Children: A Practical Guide*, London: SAGE Publications Ltd.

Osgood, J. (2006) 'Childcare Workforce Reform in England and 'The Early Years Professional': A Critical Discourse Analysis', *Journal of Education Policy*, 24(6), pp. 733–751.

Peoples, K. (2021) *How to Write a Phenomenological Dissertation: A Step-by-Step Guide*, London: SAGE Publications Ltd.

Powell, S. (2010) 'Hide and Seek: Values in Early Childhood Education and Care', *British Journal of Educational Studies*, 58(2), pp. 213–229.

Roberts-Holmes, G. and Bradbury, A. (2016) 'The Datafication of Early Years Education and Its Impact upon Pedagogy', *Improving Schools*, 19(2), pp. 119–128.

Roberts-Holmes, G. (2020) 'Towards a Pluralist and Participatory Accountability', in Cameron, C. and Moss, P. (eds.), *Transforming Early Childhood in England: Towards a Democratic Education*, London: UCL Press, pp. 170–187.

Roulston, K. (2001) 'Data Analysis and "Theorizing as Ideology"', *Qualitative Research*, 1(3), pp. 279–302.

Rudoe, N. (2020) '"We Believe in Every Child as an Individual": Nursery School Head Teachers' Understandings of Quality in Early Years Education', *British Educational Research Journal*, 46(5), pp. 1012–1025.

Siraj-Blatchford, I. et al. (2002) *Researching Effective Pedagogy in the Early Years (REPEY)*, London: Queen's Printer.

Smith, J.A., Flowers, P. and Larkin, M. (2009) *Interpretative Phenomenological Analysis: Theory, Method and Research*, London: SAGE Publications Ltd.

Sylva, K., Melhuish, E., Sammons, P., Siraj-Blatchford, I. and Taggart, B. (2004) *The Effective Provision of Preschool Education (EPPE) Project Technical Paper 12 – The Final Report: Effective Preschool Education*, London: DfES.

Wästerfors, D., Åkerström, M. and Jacobsson, K. (2013) 'Reanalysis of Qualitative Data', in Flick, U. (ed.), *The SAGE Handbook of Qualitative Data Analysis*, London: SAGE Publications Ltd., pp. 467–480.

11
RECOGNISING AND SURVIVING POVERTY WITHIN EARLY CHILDHOOD PRACTICE

Sandra Lyndon

Introduction

Levels of poverty in the UK are increasingly concerning. The Institute for Fiscal Studies (IFS) predicts that by 2022 child poverty rates will have risen to nearly 40% (Hood and Waters, 2017). Poverty has a significant impact on children's life chances with gaps in health and educational attainment increasing as children get older. Government policies to alleviate childhood poverty have largely failed and in some cases contributed to increased family debt (Paull et al., 2017; House of Commons Education Committee, HCEC, 2019; Department for Work and Pensions, DWP, 2021). Quality early childhood education and care have a positive impact on the life chances for children affected by poverty (HCEC, 2019). However, cuts to children's services due to austerity measures, Brexit and COVID-19 have resulted in a crisis in early years provision in recent years. Despite being well positioned to support families in poverty, one in ten of the UK childcare workforce live in poverty themselves (Crown, 2019), presenting a 'poverty paradox'. This chapter interrogates how early years practitioners living in poverty themselves can alleviate poverty of others.

I approach the discussion of child poverty from multiple positions. As a senior lecturer at a small university teaching across several Early Childhood programmes, part of my role is preparing students for working with children living in poverty. I am also an Early Childhood Practitioner (ECP), working for many years as a teacher and then an educational psychologist; and in this role I witnessed first-hand how poverty affects the lives of young children and their families. My data emerges from a qualitative narrative study with ECPs living and working in the South-East of England, exploring their understandings of poverty and the children and families they work with. 'Othering' discourses of poverty are interrogated and the extent to which ECPs are able to resist, contest or reproduce these.

DOI: 10.4324/9781003206262-12

The context of poverty in the UK

Recent figures suggest that 31% of children in the UK are living in relative poverty (DWP, 2021). The UN Special Rapporteur on extreme poverty and human rights described the situation as, 'not just a disgrace, but a social calamity and economic disaster, all rolled into one' (Alston, 2018, p. 1). Since COVID-19 in particular, the lives of low-income families and children have become increasingly difficult, due to a rise in living costs, additional caring responsibilities, unemployment and problems accessing benefits (Child Poverty Action Group, CAPG, 2020). More families have fallen into poverty and there has been a significant increase in the number of families receiving benefits (Blundell et al., 2021). An exponential rise in food bank use in the UK reflects the increase in families who struggle to provide their children with basic necessities (The Trussell Trust, 2020). Together with the impact of Brexit (the UK's exit from the European Union), it is likely that child poverty rates will be further affected, rising markedly beyond the figures predicted pre-COVID-19, unless there is continued and further support for families on lower incomes (Hood and Waters, 2017; Barnard et al., 2018; Joseph Rowntree Foundation, 2021).

Many families in the UK are vulnerable to poverty; however, some are more at risk than others. Lone parents have the highest poverty rate among working-age adults, with 43% living in poverty (DWP, 2021). Family poverty is highly gendered. Research suggests that 90% of lone parents are women and that they are more at risk due to inequality in work opportunities, low pay, and childcare costs (Millar and Ridge, 2013; Alston, 2018; DWP, 2021). Rather than acknowledging and tackling structural inequalities such as low pay and gender, the problem of poverty is often placed on the individual as something for them to ameliorate (Bullen and Kenway, 2006). Historically, parents experiencing poverty have been identified within government policy as being responsible for their 'troubles' and part of a 'cycle of deprivation', transmitting poverty to their children via poor parenting, lifestyles and values (Welshman, 2006; Boddy et al., 2016). Lister (2015) states that discourses which 'blame' individuals for their own circumstances serve to 'other' and legitimise the stigmatisation of those in poverty. 'Othering' results in the poor being 'blamed' for their own and societies' problems whilst legitimising the position and privilege of the 'non-poor' (Lister, 2004). Tyler (2008) argues that women – particularly lone mothers – are most likely to be 'othered' through punitive benefit policies as well as pathologizing media constructs.

The impact of poverty on children's lives

The effect of poverty on children's lives is significant and pervasive. Ridge's (2011) review of qualitative research with low-income children in the UK concluded that poverty affects every aspect of children's lives, including: economic and material deprivation, social relationships, well-being and family life, housing and homelessness, and education. Cooper and Stewart's (2018) international systematic review found that low income has a strong and detrimental impact on children's health and education. Social aspects of poverty, such as 'stigma, shame, sadness and the fear of being identified or isolated for being different', are often overlooked, despite being important issues for children (Ridge, 2011, p. 82) and affecting their well-being. For example, by age 14 children living in low-income families are four times more likely to experience emotional and behavioural difficulties (Rees, 2019). There is already a significant gap in children's educational attainment by the age of five, with those from low-income families and living in less affluent areas underperforming compared to their peers; this pattern continues throughout children's education (Department for Education, DfE, 2014; Social Mobility Commission [SMC], 2017). Despite poverty being one of the most serious determinants of educational outcomes, the DfE no longer reports on this variable in their annual EYFS profile results in England, perhaps suggesting that narrowing the gap for children in the early years has become less of a priority (DfE, 2019a).

The role of Early Childhood Education and Care in alleviating poverty

Early Childhood Education and Care (ECEC) provision plays a significant role, in addressing the effects of poverty in Early Childhood. In the late 1990s Sure Start Children Centres (SSCCs), with fully integrated universal services, were initially established in areas of deprivation and later extended to all areas. The core purpose of SSCCs was to 'improve outcomes for young children and their families and reduce inequalities between families in greatest need and their peers' (DfE, 2013, p. 7). The rationale for SSCCs is supported by evidence from the Effective Provision of Pre-School Education (EPPE) longitudinal study, which investigated the attainment and development of children between the ages of three to seven years. The study found that 'children from families on low incomes benefit significantly from good quality pre-school experiences' (Sylva et al., 2004, p. 1). SSCCs worked together with the statutory, voluntary, private and independent ECEC sector to provide support services for children and families (DfES, 2006). Evaluation of the outcomes of Children's Centres suggest that there were positive outcomes for children's behaviour and social development (Sammons et al., 2015).

With a change in government in 2010 the focus of SSCCs shifted from providing universal services for all children and families to targeted services for those in greatest need (DfE, 2013). Funding for public services and local authority budgets were significantly reduced under austerity measures, and as a result many local authorities struggled to maintain the services provided by SSCCs (Baldock et al., 2013). As a consequence, the number of SSCCs decreased from 3,620 in 2010 to 2,350 in June 2019, a reduction of over 30%, with those in areas of high deprivation most affected (DfE, 2019b). In their analysis of data between 2014 and 2019, *Action for Children* (2019) reported that the number of families and children accessing SSCCs had decreased by 10%. They found that where Children's Centre use was lower, the attainment gap between low-income children and their peers increased by 0.3% by the age of five, and where usage was higher, the gap decreased by 0.5%. Although these percentages are small, the closure of Children's Centres may be significant in explaining why children's outcomes improve in some areas and not others (*Action for Children*, 2019).

During the COVID-19 pandemic low-income families were disproportionately affected, widening the gap between rich and poor (Whitehead et al., 2021). In response to increased inequality, the government published *The Best Start for Life: A Vision for the 1,001 Critical Days* (HM Government, 2021), which set out its agenda for 'levelling up' economic opportunity in England. The report proposes creating 'Local Family Hubs', building on the work of Children's Centres, to provide integrated services for families and children from birth to nineteen. Whilst the proposals are arguably a positive move, concerns have been raised about how the work of 'Local Family Hubs' will be funded, particularly in light of ongoing cuts to budgets for children's services (UK Parliament, 2019; Hill, 2021). The proposals also beg the question of why funding for SSCCs has been cut over the past ten years when evidence indicates that intervention in the early years provides savings in the longer term (Allen, 2011).

SSCCs are not the only part of the ECEC sector to be impacted. Maintained Nursery Schools (MNSs), funded by local authorities, have worked together with SSCCs, often on co-located sites, to provide high quality education and integrated services for children, families and other local providers (Early Education, 2014). Most are found in the most deprived areas and evidence indicates that they have been successful in narrowing the attainment gap (Early Education, 2015). Since 1980 a third of MNSs have closed and only 389 remain (Early Education, 2020). Less government funding and increased staffing costs have resulted in many of the remaining MNSs reducing teaching staff to minimum numbers. Additional costs incurred during the pandemic are likely to result in many nursery schools falling into deficit, as unlike other age phases they have not been able to access additional funding from the government during this time (Early Education, 2020).

The majority of ECEC provision in the UK is provided by the Private, Voluntary and Independent (PVI) sector, with many settings providing all year-round care and education (Rutter and the Family Childcare Trust, 2017). An integral component of government policy to address poverty in early childhood is providing children with a high-quality early education as well as supporting parents into paid work. In 2006, funded education for 'disadvantaged' two-year-olds was introduced to improve outcomes for children and to close the gap by the children who started school (Gibb et al., 2011). In September 2017 the government launched 'free' 30 hours education and care for children aged three to four years (*DfE*, 2018). The policy was designed to support parents into work and increase the numbers of hours parents were able to work. A major issue with the policy has been the low funding from central government which has impacted on the number of providers willing to make the offer due to fiscal restraints (Paull et al., 2017). The National Day Nursery Association (NDNA, 2019) reported that since the policy was introduced the number of nurseries which have closed in England has increased by 153%, nearly a third of these in the most deprived areas.

The role of the early childhood practitioner in alleviating poverty and the 'poverty paradox'

ECPs are integral to the delivery of early years policy and improving outcomes for children and families who have been affected by poverty (Solvason, Webb and Sutton-Tsang, 2020a). Evidence suggests that ECPs can make a significant difference to closing the educational gap for children (Solvason, Webb and Sutton-Tsang, 2020b). Findings from the EPPE study suggest that ECPs with higher qualifications and those that provide 'warm interactive relationships with children' increase the quality of provision and have the most impact on children's attainment (Sylva et al., 2004, p. ii). However, despite evidence that a 'quality' ECEC workforce can make a significant difference for children and families living in poverty, ECPs have been subject to what can be described as a 'poverty paradox'. On the one hand they are charged with addressing poverty for young children and families, whilst on the other hand many ECPs are leaving the profession because of poor pay and little opportunity for progression.

Although attempts have been made to 'professionalise' the sector (see Chapter 1), parity with similar professionals has never been achieved. The SMC (2020) reports that the average wage of ECPs is well below the national minimum wage. More than 40% of ECPs claim state benefits or tax credits, a higher percentage than competing occupations such as hairdressers and beauticians (Bonetti, 2019). In a survey by Nursery World more than 10% of ECPs were living in relative poverty with a household income below 60% of the median, and many were unable to afford the basics (Crown, 2019). Consequently, the combination of poor working conditions and low wages has resulted in recruitment issues and high turnover rates, with ECPs leaving the sector for less demanding and better paid work (SMC, 2020).

Government policy does little to recognise or address how an ECP on low wages, who is also a mother, achieves work-life balance and accesses affordable childcare for her own children (Osgood, 2009). At the heart of the ECP 'poverty paradox' is a 'double bind' (Bateson et al., 1956), a situation where a person is confronted with two irreconcilable requests which cause emotional distress. On the one hand, government policy suggests that ECPs are integral to addressing child poverty (*DfE*, 2018; HM Government, 2021); however, there is little recognition or support for ECPs, resulting in a workforce which is undervalued, underfunded, poorly paid and in a state of crisis (Bonetti, 2019; Crown, 2019; SMC, 2020). This begs the question of how ECPs can address poverty for others when many are living in poverty themselves.

Researching early childhood practitioners' narratives of poverty

Several years ago I conducted a study with ECPs to investigate how they understood poverty in early childhood. The practitioners were from two MNSs, with attached Children's Centres and private daycare, in the South-East of England (Lyndon, 2019a, 2019b, 2020). The South-East of England has, overall, relative affluence compared to other parts of the country, however, both settings served localities which were in the 30% most disadvantaged areas in England (HCEC, 2013). A narrative qualitative approach was taken to explore how practitioners' understandings were shaped by discourses of poverty and their personal and professional experiences. The thirty-eight participants included Teachers (with Qualified Teacher Status); Nursery Nurses; Nursery Assistants; Family Support Workers; and Managers who took part in focus groups and some individual, semi-structured interviews. Data were analysed using a narrative approach, drawing on the work of Bamberg and Georgakopoulou's (2008) concept of 'small stories'.

The analysis revealed how practitioners' understandings of poverty were complex and nuanced. Whilst some narratives challenged a discourse of 'work pays', others fed into a moral discourse of parents constructed as 'deserving' or 'undeserving'. Analysis of practitioners' personal experiences of poverty and how this intersected with their practitioner lives afforded greater understanding of the tensions between them and the families that they work with. To protect the identity of participants all names of individuals and settings have been anonymised.

Deserving and undeserving poor

Many practitioners made moral comparisons between parents. For example, they made distinctions between those experiencing in-work poverty (living in poverty despite their paid employment) and those who had experienced unexpected events and who were living on benefits out of work. Some parents were viewed as responsible for their situation through, for example, mismanaging their money. Heather discussed how certain families prioritised 'status goods' over basic necessities:

> But I think for some [it's a] lifestyle choice, it's like they – a lot of parents live beyond their means … and it's like actually, is that a necessity? … Is that a priority to have Sky [television]? … But have you got enough food? Enough money to pay your rent?

In this example the parent is held responsible for their poverty and 'othered' for prioritising the 'wrong things'.

Parents experiencing in-work poverty were less likely to be judged or held responsible. Many practitioners challenged a discourse of 'work pays', highlighting the challenges working parents experience, as a result of low wages, limited work opportunities, prohibitive childcare and housing costs. For example, Christina commented on the challenges for lone mothers who want to work:

> The cost got too much and she ended up getting in debt and so she's ended having to move in with her parents … I mean this is a woman who obviously works so much … I mean the fees of nursery are ridiculous.

In this example, the parent is not judged and instead structural factors, such as the prohibitive cost of childcare, are constructed as the course of poverty.

In the same way parents who experienced 'unexpected events', such as bereavement, having a child with a disability, separation, or experience of domestic violence, were also less likely to be judged. One of the practitioners referred to these as 'curve balls'. For example, families who have a child with a disability are more vulnerable to poverty because caring responsibilities make it more difficult for parents to work (Marsh et al., 2017). Betty tells a story about a family who fell into poverty after having a child with a serious medical condition:

> Dad had to leave his job ... and they were trying to manage the care of their older child here and at the same time try and see their very poorly new-born baby ... transportation ... things like that ... costs were huge.

In this story the parents are not judged or shamed – instead they are constructed as 'deserving' despite their troubles.

Experiences of motherhood

A Nursery World Survey found that many ECPs with their own children choose not to access childcare for themselves because of prohibitive costs and that some struggle to provide their children with basic necessities (Gaunt, 2021). Over half the participants in my study had their own children and experienced tensions between their role as a mother and as an EC practitioner. Many were living on low incomes and discussed the challenges of caring for their children whilst also working. ECPs addressed these challenges in different ways, including becoming more qualified and gaining a higher paid job; working long hours; or doing without. Diana talked about how she kept her family financially stable by making the decision to have only one child:

> I only have one child ... because we made the decision that I needed to go back to work and actually childcare and also our housing meant that we weren't in a position to have any more and we made that decision ourselves to keep ourselves stable ... I then see families with lots and lots of children and really struggling and I ... can understand why they would want these children because ... the joy that they bring you is incredible ... I suppose there is part of me that just thinks **maybe** you could have made slightly different choices.

Diana's story highlights the difficult choices for ECPs living on low incomes. She compares her situation with that of the families she works with – perhaps judging those who choose to have 'lots of children' as lacking financial responsibility. Her story also suggests sadness and regret as she reflects on 'the joy' that having a large family can bring. Overall, her narrative illustrates tensions for Diana between her personal decisions and her professional role. On the one hand she positions herself as a responsible mother (making a moral choice to only have one child), whilst on the other she positions herself as a professional caring for the multiple children of a mother who made quite different choices.

Experiencing the shame of poverty

Although many ECPs discussed financial restraint impacting at different points in their lives, only one talked about living in extreme poverty. Audrey was based in one of the Children's Centres and worked directly with children and families. As a young mother she and her family had experienced homelessness, and throughout her interview she referred to this and reflected on how those living in poverty experience shame and stigma. She talked about her experience of school non-uniform day:

> You know, when I was on benefits and my kids were at school, I used to feel like if they had a non-uniform day, I had to go out and buy my kids new clothes … and leave myself really short for the rest of the week … 'cause I used to think, 'I don't want everyone looking at my kids thinking we're tramps. I don't want everyone judging me and thinking that I don't look after my kids 'cause I haven't got a job'.

Audrey's lived experience affords her greater insight into how those in poverty are judged and shamed. Chase and Walker (2012) found that those living in poverty experience internal and external judgement; they are both shamed by others for being poor as well as feeling shame. Consequently, some try to avoid humiliation and judgement by concealing their poverty through unnecessary expenditure such as that mentioned above and through not asking for help (Chase and Walker, 2012). The underlying message of Audrey's story is that she would rather go without than risk her children being judged for being poor.

Concluding thoughts

Overall, the ECPs' understandings of poverty were nuanced and complex and their narratives intersected in intricate ways with social class, gender and race (see Lyndon, 2019a, 2019b, 2020). However, pervasive across their narratives was a complexity of moral discourses which, to some extent, served to 'other' those in poverty through a process of social distancing and individualisation. Parents who were experiencing in-work poverty were less likely to be judged and more likely to be constructed as 'hard working' and doing their best to support their children, whilst those living on benefits were more likely to be judged in terms of lifestyle choices, such as prioritising the 'wrong' things. Broadly ECPs understood poverty in terms of 'deserving' or 'undeserving' poor; with some families constructed as more deserving than others.

Attention to ECP's professional and personal lives affords a greater understanding of the 'poverty paradox', or how ECPs are expected to address poverty for the children and families they work with when many are living in poverty themselves. Many ECPs mentioned financial challenges and highlighted issues of low pay, high childcare costs and precarious work. This perhaps explains why they were less likely to judge working parents, as many were experiencing similar challenges in their own lives. ECPs responses to their own circumstances were individualised. Some became more qualified; gained a higher paid job; worked long hours or did without, demonstrating moral restraint, whereas others tried to hide or deny their poverty. However, despite personal struggles with poverty as a result of their role, they were still committed wholeheartedly to improving the lives of children and families they worked with.

In seeking a solution to the 'poverty paradox', there are two fundamental questions to consider:

- How do ECPs address issues of inequality and lack of funding within the ECEC sector?
- How do ECPs challenge attitudes towards those living in poverty?

Pressure is mounting to review early years policy and prevent the further closure of settings. In an inquiry into financial sustainability conducted by the All Party Parliamentary Group (APPG, 2021), 72% of parents said they would struggle to work if they were unable to access early years settings. Most of the parents taking part in the survey were mothers, suggesting that underfunding ECEC provision would contribute further to inequalities for women. In light of the findings, the chair of the APPG and chief executive of the NDNA asked the government to properly fund the ECEC sector (Children and Young People Now, 2021). Arguably, if the government is serious about 'levelling up', then a multi-pronged approach is needed. This needs to address issues of low pay; progression; and affordable and accessible training and qualification routes for ECPs; affordable ECEC provision for parents; and sustainable funding for the maintained and PVI sectors. A stronger, more coordinated voice would enable those working within the sector to exert greater influence on government policy.

One way of challenging negative attitudes to those in poverty is to listen to and understand those who are experiencing it (Solvason et al., 2020a). Many ECPs are in similar financial circumstances to the families they work with. However, my findings suggest that ECPs find it difficult to empathise with all families, judging some as responsible for their own poverty and 'undeserving'. A way of addressing the shame of poverty is to embrace a counter discourse of human rights based on recognition and respect (Lister, 2015). Hearing and listening to the voices of families who have experienced poverty and involving them in the training and development of ECPs could help to 'shame-proof' ECEC practice. As O'Hara (2020) states, we need to listen to experts in the field, such as those who have experienced poverty; and rather than shaming the poor start to shame those in positions of power and privilege.

> **REFLECTIVE POINTS**
>
> Consider your experience of working with children and families in poverty. Is there anything discussed in this chapter which particularly chimes with your experience?
>
> - How do you understand the causes of poverty: for example, to what extent is it caused by 'life-style' choices, lack of money or inequalities within society? How are these understandings shaped by your practitioner and/or personal experience?
> - How might the 'poverty paradox' be resolved? Are there ways that ECPs could have a stronger voice and challenge issues of inequality and a lack of funding within the sector?
> - Consider ways that ECEC settings might better support children and families in poverty.

References

All Party Parliamentary Group [APPG] (2021). *Steps to sustainability – a report by the APPG for childcare and early education*. https://connectpa.co.uk/wp-content/uploads/2019/07/Steps-to-sustainability-report.pdf

Action for Children (2019). *Closed doors report*. https://www.actionforchildren.org.uk/our-work-and-impact/policy-work-campaigns-and-research/policy-reports/closed-doors/

Allen, G. (2011). *Early intervention: The next steps*. https://www.gov.uk/government/publications/early-intervention-the-next-steps--2

Alston, P. (2018). *Statement on visit to the United Kingdom, by Professor Philip Alston, United Nations special rapporteur on extreme poverty and human rights*. https://www.ohchr.org/EN/NewsEvents/Pages/DisplayNews.aspx?NewsID=23881&LangID=E

Baldock, P., Fitzgerald, D. and Kay, J. (2013). *Understanding early years policy* (3rd ed.) London: Sage.

Bamberg, M. and Georgakopoulou, A. (2008) 'Small stories as a new perspective in narrative and identity analysis', *Text & Talk*, 28(3): 377–396.

Barnard, H., Heykoop, L. and Kumar, A. (2018). *How could Brexit affect poverty in the UK?* https://www.jrf.org.uk/sites/default/files/jrf/files-research/briefing_how_could_brexit_affect_poverty_in_the_uk_0.pdf

Bateson, G., Jackson, D., Haley, J. and Weakland, J. (1956). 'Toward a theory of schizophrenia', *Behavioural Science*, 1(4): 251–264.

Blundell, R., Cribb, J., McNally, S., Warwick, R. and Xu, X. (2021). *Inequalities in education, skills, and incomes in the UK: The implications of the COVID-19 pandemic*. https://www.ifs.org.uk/publications/15380

Boddy, J., Statham, J., Warwick, I., Hollingworth, K. and Spencer, G. (2016). 'What kind of trouble? Meeting the health needs of 'Troubled Families' through intensive family support', *Social Policy and Society*, 15(2): 275–288.

Bonetti, S. (2019). *The early years workforce in England.* https://epi.org.uk/publications-and-research/the-early-years-workforce-in-england/

Bullen, E. and Kenway, J. (2006). 'Subcultural capital and the female "underclass"? A feminist response to an underclass discourse', *Journal of Youth Studies*, 7(2): 141–153.

Chase, E. and Walker, R. (2012). 'The co-construction of shame in the context of poverty: Beyond a threat to the social bond', *Sociology*, 47(4): 739–754.

Children and Young People Now (2021). *Early years funding levels not sustainable, MPs warn.* https://www.cypnow.co.uk/news/article/early-years-funding-levels-not-sustainable-mps-warn

Child Poverty Action Group (CPAG) (2020). *Poverty in the pandemic: An update on the impact of coronavirus on low-income families and children.* https://cpag.org.uk/policy-and-campaigns/report/poverty-pandemic-update-impact-coronavirus-low-income-families-and

Cooper, K. and Stewart, K. (2018). *The importance of income for children and families: An updated review of the evidence.* https://cpag.org.uk/welfare-rights/resources/article/importance-income-children-and-families-updated-review-evidence

Crown, H. (2019). *Working poverty, childcare's dirty secret, Nursery World.* https://www.nurseryworld.co.uk/news/article/exclusive-working-poverty-childcare-practitioners-childcare-s-dirty-secret

Department for Education and Skills [DfES] (2006). *SureStart children's centres practice guidance.* https://www.inclusivechoice.com/Sure%20start%20Children%E2%80%99s%20Centres%20Practice%20Guidance%20(white%20book).pdf

Department for Education [DfE] (2013). *Sure start children's centres statutory guidance*, Report No. DFE-00314-2013. London: Department for Education. https://www.gov.uk/government/uploads/system/uploads/attachment_data/file/273768/childrens_centre_stat_guidance_april_2013.pdf

Department for Education [DfE] (2014). *Statistical first release: Early years foundation stage profile results in England, 2013/14.* https://www.gov.uk/government/uploads/system/uploads/attachment_data/file/364021/SFR39_2014_Text.pdf

Department for Education [DfE] (2018). *Early years entitlements: Operational guidance for local authorities and providers.* https://www.gov.uk/government/publications/30-hours-free-childcare-la-and-early-years-provider-guide

Department for Education [DfE] (2019a). *Early years foundation stage profile in England, 2019.* https://www.gov.uk/government/statistics/early-years-foundation-stage-profile-results-2018-to-2019

Department for Education [DfE] (2019b). *Number of children's centres, 2003 to 2019 – Annual figures for the number of children's centres from 2003 to 2019 Ad-hoc Notice.* https://assets.publishing.service.gov.uk/government/uploads/system/uploads/attachment_data/file/844752/Number_of_Children_s_Centres_2003_to_2019_Nov2019.pdf

Department for Work and Pensions [DWP] (2021). *Households below average income: An analysis of the income distribution FYE 1995 to FYE 2020.* https://www.gov.uk/government/statistics/households-below-average-income-for-financial-years-ending-1995-to-2020/households-below-average-income-an-analysis-of-the-income-distribution-fye-1995-to-fye-2020

Early Education (2014). *Maintained nursery schools: Hubs for quality in the early years.* https://www.early-education.org.uk/sites/default/files/NS%20Surveys%20report_lo-res.pdf

Early Education (2015). *Maintained nursery schools: The state of play report, March 2015.* https://www.earlyeducation.org.uk/sites/default/files/Nursery%20Schools%20State%20of%20Play%20Report%20final%20print.pdf

Early Education (2020). *Maintained nursery schools and COVID-19: Vital community services on a cliff-edge.* https://early-education.org.uk/sites/default/files/The%20impact%20of%20COVID-19%20on%20MNS.pdf

Gaunt, C. (2021). *Coronavirus: Nurseries 'ignored' by government in row over reopening schools.* https://www.nurseryworld.co.uk/news/article/coronavirus-nurseries-ignored-by-government-in-row-over-reopening-schools

Gibb, J., Jelicic, H. and La Valle, I. (2011). *Rolling out free early education for disadvantaged two year olds: an implementation study for local authorities and providers.* https://assets.publishing.service.gov.uk/government/uploads/system/uploads/attachment_data/file/181502/DFE-RR131.pdf

Hill, J. (2021) *Are 'family hubs' simply Labour's children's centres in new clothes?.* https://www.lgcplus.com/politics/lgc-briefing/are-family-hubs-simply-labours-childrens-centres-in-new-clothes-16-04-2021/

HM Government (2021). *The best start for life: A vision for the 1,001 critical days.* https://assets.publishing.service.gov.uk/government/uploads/system/uploads/attachment_data/file/973112/The_best_start_for_life_a_vision_for_the_1_001_critical_days.pdf

Hood, A. and Waters, T. (2017). *Living standards, poverty and inequality in the UK: 2017–18 to 2021–22*, Institute of Fiscal Studies. https://www.ifs.org.uk/uploads/publications/comms/R136.pdf

House of Commons Education Committee [HCEC] (2013). *Foundation years: Sure start children's centres, fifth report of session 2013–14 Volume I.* http://www.publications.parliament.uk/pa/cm201314/cmselect/cmeduc/364/364.pdf

House of Commons Education Committee [HCEC] (2019). *Tackling disadvantage in the early years.* https://publications.parliament.uk/pa/cm201719/cmselect/cmeduc/1006/1006.pdf

Joseph Rowntree Foundation [JRF] (2021). *UK poverty 2020/2021 – The leading independent report.* https://www.jrf.org.uk/report/uk-poverty-2020-21

Lister, R. (2004). *Poverty*. Cambridge: Policy Press.

Lister, R. (2015). 'To count for nothing: Poverty beyond the statistics', *Journal of the British Academy*, 3: 139–165.

Lyndon, S. (2019a) *Early years practitioners' narratives of poverty in early childhood.* Doctoral thesis, University of Sussex. http://sro.sussex.ac.uk/81407/

Lyndon, S. (2019b). 'Tangles narratives of poverty in early childhood – Othering, work, welfare and 'curveballs'', *Journal of Poverty and Social Justice*, 27(3): 389–405. DOI: 10.1332/175982719X15626279221341

Lyndon, S. (2020). 'Early years practitioners' personal and professional narratives of poverty', *International Journal of Early Years Education*. DOI: 10.1080/09669760.2020.1782175

Marsh, A., Barker, K., Ayrton, C., Treanor, M. and Haddad, M. (2017). *Poverty: the facts* (6th Ed.). London: CPAG.

Millar, J. and Ridge, T. (2013). 'Lone mothers and paid work: The family-work project', *International Review of Sociology*, 23(3): 564–577.

National Day Nursery Association [NDNA] (2019). *Nursery closures rocket by 153% since 30 'free' hour policy began.* https://www.ndna.org.uk/NDNA/News/Press_releases/2019/Nursery_closures_rocket_by_153_since_30_free_hour_policy_began.aspx

O'Hara, M. (2020). *The shame game: Overturning the toxic poverty narrative.* Bristol: Policy Press.

Osgood, J. (2009). 'Childcare workforce reform in England and the early years professional: A critical discourse analysis', *Journal of Education Policy*, 24(6): 733–751.
Paull, G., La Valle, I., Speight, S., Jones, H. and White, C. (2017). *Evaluation of early implementation of 30 hours free childcare. Research Report*. https://www.gov.uk/government/uploads/system/uploads/attachment_data/file/629460/Evaluation_of_early_implementation_of_30_hours_free_childcare_.pdf
Rees, G. (2019). *Poverty and children's wellbeing at 14 years old*. https://cpag.org.uk/welfare-rights/resources/article/poverty-and-children%E2%80%99s-wellbeing-14-years-old
Ridge, T. (2011). 'The everyday costs of poverty in childhood: A review of qualitative research exploring the lives and experiences of low-income children in the UK', *Children and Society*, 25(1): 73–84.
Rutter and Family and Childcare Trust (2017). *Understanding the childcare provider market: Implications for educational suppliers.* http://docplayer.net/18754960-Understanding-the-childcare-provider-market-implications-for-educational-suppliers-jill-rutter-family-and-childcare-trust.html
Sammons, P., Hall, J., Smees, R., Goff, J. with Sylva, K., Smith, T., Evangelou, M., Eisenstadt, N. and Smith, G. (2015). *The impact of children's centres: studying the effects of children's centres in promoting better outcomes for young children and their families Evaluation of Children's Centres in England (ECCE, Strand 4) Research report December 2015.* https://www.gov.uk/government/uploads/system/uploads/attachment_data/file/485346/DFE-RR495_Evaluation_of_children_s_centres_in_England__the_impact_of_children_s_centres.pdf
Social Mobility Commission (2017). *Time for change: An assessment of government policies on social mobility.* https://www.gov.uk/government/uploads/system/uploads/attachment_data/file/622214/Time_for_Change_report_-_An_assessement_of_government_policies_on_social_mobility_1997-2017.pdf
Social Mobility Commission (2020). *The stability of the early years workforce in England – an examination of national, regional and organisational barriers.* https://www.gov.uk/government/publications/the-stability-of-the-early-years-workforce-in-england
Solvason, C., Webb, R. and Sutton-Tsang, S. (2020a) *Evidencing the effects of maintained nursery schools' roles in Early Years sector improvements.* https://tactic.org.uk/research/
Solvason, C., Webb, R. and Sutton-Tsang, S. (2020b) 'What is left…? The implications of losing Maintained Nursery Schools for vulnerable children and families in England', *Children and Society*, 35(1): 75–89.
Sylva, K., Melhuish, E., Sammons, P., Siraj-Blatchford, I. and Taggart, B. (2004). *Technical Paper 12 – The final report: Effective pre-School education.* https://discovery.ucl.ac.uk/id/eprint/10005308/
The Trussell Trust (2020). *The impact of covid-19 on food banks report.* www.trusselltrust.org/wp-content/uploads/sites/2/2020/09/the-impact-of-covid-19-on-food-banks-report.pdf
Tyler, I. (2008). 'Chav Mum Chav Scum', *Feminist Media Studies*, 8(1): 17–34.
UK Parliament (2019). *Early years Family support, volume 663: debated on Tuesday 16 July 2019.* https://hansard.parliament.uk/commons/2019-07-16/debates/5C7FA151-A4F1-4F0F-88F1-5A66A7F8F060/EarlyYearsFamilySupport
Welshman, J. (2006). 'From the cycle of deprivation to social exclusion: Five continuities', *The Political Quarterly*, 77(4): 475–484.
Whitehead, M., Taylor-Robinson, D. and Barr, B. (2021). 'Poverty, health and covid-19', *British Medical Journal*. DOI: 10.1136/bmj.n376. PMID: 33579719.

CONCLUSION

Carla Solvason and Rebecca Webb

At the risk of sounding twee, working on this edited volume has been an honour and a privilege. To have the opportunity to be reminded of the diverse and extraordinary talents of the Early Childhood Practitioner (ECP), whilst working alongside colleagues who passionately support the incredible practice going on in the field, has been a celebratory opportunity for us, and, we hope, for you too, in your reading of it. Through these individual narratives, we have seen a picture emerge of the Early Childhood Practitioner, curtailed by the belittling gendered and classist assumptions surrounding the education and care of young children that endure. Despite attempts to designate status through various graduate training routes, we have seen how this image of the education practitioner who is 'less than' persists. Despite the raft of research advocating the impacts that early education can have on later life chances, the multifaceted ECP continues to earn considerably less than, and works more informally and precariously than, counterparts within the 5-18 formal school sector.

In the early chapters of this book, we shared conceptual and empirical examples that pay attention to, and celebrate, micro contexts of practice and that reveal the range of skills, capabilities and knowledges of ECPs. Despite different roles, rankings and rewards within the private, voluntary and independent sectors of Early Childhood Education and Care (ECEC), we have heard how ECPs create inclusive environments for the thriving of young children and their families. These are thoughtful environments where the care and safety of children are at the very heart of all that they do – environments where the significant role of the parent as primary caregiver and first educator is respected and encouraged. They are also spaces where knowledges and understandings of the child are shared and really *heard* with the wellbeing of the child at the heart of positive relationships.

The subsequent chapters explore the significance of specialist expertise in areas that can become increasingly side-lined, or viewed as problematic, as children progress through the educational system. The sensitivity required of the ECP is taken up in a chapter that delves into the empathetic approach that ECPs take toward the children and families that they work with; whilst also warning us of the toll that this can take upon the wellbeing of the practitioner. And in the chapter that follows this we see how the diversity and challenge of a spectrum of particular learning needs and disabilites is embraced as a learning opportunity for reflective ECPs.

The next group of chapters looked at aspects of ECP expertise that focus upon formations of the holistic and relational child in a highly material world. This is a child subject who should be encouraged to follow their own pathways to discovering and understanding rather than being forced to follow narrow, pre-prescribed routes leading to assumed destinations. This is a child subject who is part of a world that stretches beyond families, homes and educational settings to the natural world beyond; a child who is aware of and who takes responsibility for living animals, no matter how small; and a child who should be supported by ECPs, to unleash their unlimited creative potential.

The final chapters of this book see authors 're-imagine' the role of the ECP in different ways, drawing on different theoretical conceptualisations that encourage readers to think about the ECP beyond the limitations of a reductionist configuration. This requires considering the practitioner as a creative, reflective and thoughtful subject who is capable of innovative approaches that challenge norms of pedagogical practices that adhere relentlessly to preplanned activities with predefined outcomes. This means rethinking our conception of what a quality interaction in ECEC might present. Finally, we have engaged with a chapter that has made us stop and consider the irony of those working on minimum wage, often forced to take on additional employment to supplement their meagre income, being viewed as the 'solution' to cycles of poverty and deprivation witnessed with early childhood education and care.

The ECP is multifaceted, complex and resilient and has persistently fought to shape more appropriate agendas for ECEC rather than just conforming to prescribed (and often inappropriate) policy and metrics. Working on this book has reminded us of the extreme complexity found in so much of EC practice – a practice that is hugely subjective, reactive to context and the individual needs therein. It is a practice that demonstrates sensitive awareness of the intricacy and diversity of the lives encountered in settings (rather than trying to funnel individuals into normative 'achievable aims') that makes EC practice so rich, so complex and so valuable … and so much 'more than' the standardising education delivered in other age phases. Unfortunately, it is also what makes it so difficult for those who cannot grasp this complexity to recognise its worth.

The sensitive, empathetic and responsive ECP is cast adrift in a sea of positivist educational ideas expecting normative outcomes. The ECP, fully aware of the constructivist reality of education and the uniqueness of each and every child and family, is able to respond chameleon-like to the needs of all. And it is this very quality, embodying responsiveness, reflectivity and adaptability that makes the role of the ECP so very difficult to pin down, and which, ultimately, leads to it being dismissed by those who fail to understand it. So, thank you for joining us in this celebration of the multifaceted and multi-talented Early Childhood Practitioner. We are aware that there are many, many more qualities to this role that we have not been able to fit in this short volume, and we hope that you will also tell the many stories that still need to be told.

INDEX

accountability 13, 19, 29, 117–119
All our futures see National Advisory Committee for Creative and Cultural Education
alternative pedagogies 67–68
assessment: of learning 67–68, 118–119; for SEND 55–56
attainment gap 18, 56, 126
attainment targets *see* outcomes
austerity measures 58, 123, 125
autonomy 13, 14, 65, 118

Birth to Five Matters 74, 113, 119
Birth to Three Matters 10

care, inter-relationship with education 6–7, 66–67, 69–70
characteristics of effective learning, 87, 93
childcare 5, 12
Childcare Act (2006) 6
child-initiated learning, 112
childminders 7
Children and Families Act 55
Children's Centres 125–126
Children's Workforce Development Council (CWDC) 10
Children's Workforce Strategy 68
compassion 44
continuing professional development (CPD) 57
COVID-19 19, 31, 124, 126
creative learning 89
creative pedagogies 89
creative thinking 88–89

creativity: definitions of 87–88; and play 88–89; and science 88; teaching creativity 89, 95
critical thinking: by adults 19–20, 22–24, 64; by children 88, 93, 95
curriculum 5, 13, 58, 67–68
Curriculum Guidance for the Foundation Stage 10

data-driven pedagogy 13, 66, 118
democratic deficit, 14
democratic engagement 100–101
Denmark 67
developmentally-appropriate practice (DAP) 66–67
development goals *see* outcomes
Development Matters 74, 83, 99, 111–112
disadvantaged children and families 9, 18, 56, 65–66, 94, 126

early childhood sector: investment in 5, 9, 65, 125–126; purpose of 1; role in responding to disadvantage 9–10, 33, 56–58, 125–126
early intervention 9, 18–19, 55, 126
Early Years Foundation Stage (EYFS) 10, 30, 55, 64–65, 74
Early Years Professional Status (EYPS) 10–11
Early Years Teachers 11
Early Years Workforce Commission 12
Early Years Workforce Strategy 11, 56
Educational outcomes *see* outcomes
Effective Pedagogy (EPPE) Project 8–9, 65, 112, 125, 127

emotional labour 7, 38, 45
empathic distress 44–47
empathy: advanced empathy skills 42–44; and compassion 44; definition of 41–42; and gender 48; with parents 34–35
environmental sustainability 81, 83, 99
ethic of care 8, 13, 43, 69
Every Child Matters 10, 30
EYFS profile 125

Froebel, F 7
funding 12, 56–57, 60, 125–126

gender 7–8, 48, 77
graduate staff 8–10

health promotion 21
home-school relationships 29–31, 60
human capital 9, 13

inclusion 54–55
individual education and health-care plans (IHCP) 59
integrated services 10, 19, 55, 125–126
integration 54–56
interactions: as evidence 117–119; measuring 114–115; and outcomes 112–113, 115–116; social purpose of 114–115

job satisfaction 47–48
justice, children's concepts of 75, 77–78, 83

key worker system 21
kindness 37

learning environment 91–92
life chances 19, 123, 126
life course approach 19–21
listening 21, 35–36, 43, 75, 100–101, 113
lone parents 124

maintained nursery schools (MNS) 31, 56–58, 60–61, 126
maternalism 7
measurable outcomes *see* outcomes
Millennium Cohort Study 9
models of disability 54
moral codes 75, 83
moral purpose 8, 13
More Great Childcare 11
more knowledgeable other (MKO) 78

National Advisory Committee for Creative and Cultural Education (NACCCE) 88–89

National Professional Qualifications Framework for Early Years Leadership 11–12
nature: benefits for children 74; children's engagement with 74–75, 78, 80, 83–84; children's understanding of 77, 83; and ethics 73–74, 82–83
neo-liberalism 9, 12, 14, 65
New Zealand 67
Northern Ireland 28
Nutbrown Review 2, 10

Ofsted 66, 95, 112, 118
Othering 10, 64, 66, 69, 123–124
outcomes; *see also* targets; accountability for 5, 115, 117, 119; and development 21, 29, 112–113, 125–126; measurable 9, 30, 65–66, 69, 111, 115; prescribed 13, 67, 113; quality, as measure of 12, 65, 111–115, 117

parent partnership 29–31
parents: building trust with 35; as customers 29; listening to 35–36; role and responsibilities of 29–30
pedagogical documentation 68, 75
pedagogical knowledge 9, 63, 69
pedagogical leadership 10
pedagogical values 13, 118
pedagogy: alternative pedagogies 67–68; common worlds pedagogy 73; creative pedagogies 89; as dominant discourse 63–64; 'not knowing' pedagogy 100, 104–105; nurturing pedagogies 69–70; and performance 65; social pedagogy 21
performativity 13, 117
play-based learning 7, 11, 66, 68–69, 75, 78–80
Plowden Report 28
policy objectives 5, 9, 14, 19, 60, 111, 123, 126
political ideology 11, 13–14, 63, 131
possibility thinking 88, 95
post-humanistic perspectives 73, 80, 83
poverty: discourses of 128–129; ECEC and 29, 125–126; gendered nature of 124; impact on children of 124–125; increasing levels of 124; and shame 130
poverty paradox 127
private, voluntary and independent (PVI) sector 9–10, 126, 131
professionalisation 7–8, 10–12, 18, 63, 127
professionalism 6–8, 12–14, 66
professional love 127
public services, funding of 5, 125–126

qualifications 8–9, 100
qualified teacher status (QTS) 11–12
quality 12, 19, 65, 111–115, 118

recruitment and retention 12, 127
reflection 8, 13–14, 22, 49, 101, 105
Reggio Emilia 67–68, 101, 107
regimes of truth 63–64
regulatory standards and requirements 14, 24, 69, 118; *see also* statutory policies and frameworks
Researching Effective Pedagogy in the Early Years (REPEY) 112
resources 91–92, 99, 107
risk taking 88–90, 95, 108
Rumbold Report 8

safeguarding: child-centred approach to 19, 36; and children's rights 21; definition of 18; and practitioner identity 24
schoolification, 66, 68–69
school-readiness 13, 66, 112
Scotland 28
serious case reviews 19
social disadvantage and deprivation 9, 33, 57, 65–66, 94–95, 126
social inequality 20, 126
socialisation 100
social justice 19–20, 22
social pedagogues 21–22, 67–68
Special Educational Needs and Disability Act (SENDA) 54
Special Educational Needs and Disability Code of Practice, The 55
special educational needs and disability (SEND): identification of 55–56; and mainstream entitlement 54–55; practitioner expertise in 56, 59; and relationships with parents 34–35, 54
specialised knowledge 8, 13–14, 63, 65
special schools 34–35, 55
Start Right Report 8
statutory policies and frameworks 19, 28, 64, 66, 69, 74, 99–100, 111–112; *see also* regulatory requirements
subjectivity 100, 115
Sure Start 10, 125–126
sustainability: environmental 81, 83, 99; financial 56–57, 60, 125–126, 131; of the workforce 12, 127, 131
Sustainable Development Goals 99
sustained shared thinking (SST) 9, 78, 112, 120

targets 67, 93, 112
Teaching Standards 11
technicist practice 13, 65–66, 73
Te Whariki 68
transformative practice 99–100
transitions 20–21, 59

United Nations Rights of the Child 21, 54, 100

vertical grouping 99, 103–104

Wales 28
Warnock Report, The 54
well-being 13, 18, 47, 74, 124–125
workforce, sustainability of 12, 127, 131
working together to safeguard children 18
worms 78, 81

zone of proximal development (ZPD) 78

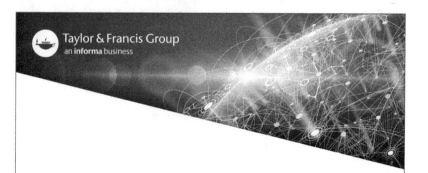